WORKERS WITHOUT BORDERS

Workers without Borders

Posted Work and Precarity in the EU

Ines Wagner

ILR Press

An imprint of Cornell University Press

Ithaca and London

First published 2018 by Cornell University Press

Printed in the United States of America

Library of Congress Cataloging-in-Publication Data

Names: Wagner, Ines, 1984– author.
Title: Workers without borders : posted work and precarity in the
    EU / Ines Wagner.
Description: Ithaca : ILR Press, an imprint of Cornell University Press,
    2018. | Includes bibliographical references and index.
Identifiers: LCCN 2018013445 (print) | LCCN 2018013885 (ebook) |
    ISBN 9781501729164 (epub/mobi) | ISBN 9781501729171 (pdf) |
    ISBN 9781501729157 (cloth : alk. paper)
Subjects: LCSH: Foreign workers—European Union countries. |
    Foreign workers—Germany. | Employee rights—European Union
    countries. | Employee rights—Germany. | Precarious employment—
    European Union countries. | Precarious employment—Germany.
Classification: LCC HD8378.5.A2 (ebook) | LCC HD8378.5.A2 W34
    2018 (print) | DDC 331.5/44094—dc23
LC record available at https://lccn.loc.gov/2018013445

Für Lore, Mama, und Tim

CONTENTS

ACKNOWLEDGMENTS

First and foremost, I am deeply grateful to the people who allowed me access to their mobility experiences for this book. Without them, this work would obviously not have been possible. Your stories and hospitality will stay with me. Second, I would like to extend my thanks to the various trade unions and works councilors who allowed me to accompany them on housing site visits and helped me set up the fieldwork, as well as the interpreters, translators, and transcribers who aided me in the development of the interviews.

It has been a pleasure to do the research for this book as part of the European Research Council project Transnational Work and the Evolution of Sovereignty (#263782) with Nathan Lillie as PI. Thanks are due specifically to Nathan Lillie, Lisa Berntsen, Sonila Danaj, Erka Çaro, Laura Mankki, and Markku Sippola. My deep appreciation also goes out to Sjoerd Beugelsdijk and the Global Economics and Management Department at the University of Groningen, as well as to Marja Keränen and the Political Science Department at the University of Jyväskylä. I had the pleasure of presenting various aspects of this work to many groups, and I am grateful for the invitations to do so. Thank you also to the many people who discussed various aspects of this work at conferences, reviewed my submissions to journals, or offered feedback on works in process. In particular, thank you to Gabriella Alberti, Magdalena Bernaciak, Andreas Bieler, Ian Bruff, Brian Burgoon, Jan Cremers, Virginia Doellgast, Jan Drahokoupil, Matthias Ebenau, Roland Erne, Ian Greer, Anke Hassel, Marco Hauptmeier, Mijke Houwerzijl, Gregory Jackson, Niilo Kauppi, Jette Steen Knudsen, Miriam Kullmann, Katja Mäkinen, Stefania Marino, Christian May, Andreas Nölke, Marko Nousiainen, Maite Tapia, and Bettina Wagner as well as various anonymous reviewers.

Apart from the university and project support already mentioned, the Max-Planck Institute for the Study of Societies in Cologne and the Wirtschafts und Sozialwissenschaftliches Institute hosted me during my fieldwork periods in Germany. Discussions with Martin Höpner, Armin Schäfer, Martin Seeliger, Benjamin Werner, Karin Schulze-Buschoff, Jutta Höhne, Martin Behrens, and Thorsten Schulten helped me think through the research design and interpretation of findings.

A conversation with Tanja Börzel several years ago planted the idea for this book. I am deeply grateful for her support as part of the mentoring program of the Ruhr University Alliance and for the valuable advice she gave me throughout our various meetings. I worked on parts of this book manuscript while I was a visiting scholar at the European University Institute in Florence. Rainer Bauböck, Doro Bohle, Claire Kilpatrick, and Sandra Engelbrecht were helpful in figuring out what was particularly interesting in my research. I am grateful for the discussions with Karen Jaehrling, Claudia Weinkopf, Gerhard Bosch, Karen Shire, Sigrid Quack, and Glaucia Peres da Silva during my work at the University of Duisburg-Essen. Moreover, I am grateful to the Institute for Social Research in Oslo and the Norwegian Research Council grant (#257603/H20) for supporting the final stages of the writing process. Fran Benson of Cornell University Press gave much valued support during the publication process, and the copyediting of Liz Schueler and production work of Karen Hwa significantly improved the text.

Several chapters in this book draw on previously published material: chapter 3, Ines Wagner, "Rule Enactment in a Pan-European Labour Market: Transnational Posted Work in the German Construction Sector," *British Journal of Industrial Relations* 53 (4): 692–710, © John Wiley & Sons Ltd/

London School of Economics 2014; chapter 4, "EU Posted Work and Transnational Action in the German Meat Industry," *Transfer: European Review of Labour and Research* 21 (2): 201–13; and chapter 5, Ines Wagner, "The Political Economy of Borders in a 'Borderless' European Labour Market," *Journal of Common Market Studies* 53 (6): 1370–85.

Finally, I thank my family and friends for their never-ending encouragement and belief in me. You are too many to list, but I want to mention Uri, my father, and my sister, Tanja, as well as Philip, Elsemieke, Jan, Daan, Anne, Sol, Lev, Hugo, Sam, Nan, Claudia, and Alex. Tim, my deepest gratitude goes to you, for always being there, for patiently listening to my endless thoughts about posted work, for waiting up late at night with a warm cup of tea after my long fieldwork trips, for critically reading my drafts, and for supporting me in every possible way. Most of all, thank you for the wondrous life outside academia, which is full of love and laughter. The research and writing of this book were interrupted twice. My mother sadly died when I started the research for this book. As a child of immigrants from Eastern Europe, she influenced my thinking on what home, mobility, and belonging mean in our society. The second, and this time pleasant, interruption to the writing process was the birth of our daughter, Lore, who is my greatest inspiration. This book is dedicated to the three of you.

Abbreviations

ANG	Arbeitgebervereinigung Nahrung und Genuss e.V. (Food and Beverage Employers' Association)
BA	Bundesagntur für Arbeit (Federal Employment Agency, Germany)
BDA	Bundesvereinigung der Deutschen Arbeitgeberverbände (Confederation of German Employers' Association)
BDS	Bundesverband der Systemgastronomie (Federal Association of System Catering)
BLL	Bund für Lebensmittelrecht und Lebensmittelkunde e.V. (German Federation for Food Law and Food Science)
BMAS	Bundesministerium für Arbeit und Soziales (Federal Ministry of Labour and Social Affairs, Germany)
BMI	Bundesministerium des Innern (Federal Ministry of the Interior, Germany)
BVE	Bundesvereinigung der Deutschen Ernährungsindustrie e.V. (Federal Association of the German Food Industry)

DEHOGA	Deutscher Hotel und Gaststättenverband (Hotel and Restaurant Association, Germany)
DGB	Deutscher Gewerkschaftsbund (German Labor Federation)
ECJ	European Court of Justice
ED	Enforcement Directive
EEA	European Economic Area
EFTA	European Free Trade Association
EMWU	European Migrant Workers Union
EU	European Union
FKS	Finanzkontrolle Schwarzarbeit (Customs Enquiries)
HDB	Hauptverband Deutsche Bauindustrie (Central Association of the German Construction Industry)
IG BAU	Industrie Gewerkschaft Bauen-Agrar-Umwelt (Industrial Union of Construction and Agriculture)
IG	Metall Industrie Gewerkschaft Metall (Industrial Union of Metalworkers)
IGZ	Interessengemeinschaft Deutscher Zeitarbeitsunternehmen (Association of the German Temporary Work Association)
ILO	International Labour Organization
NGG	Nahrung-Genuss-Gaststätten (Food, Beverages and Catering Union)
NGO	Nongovernmental Organization
OECD	Organisation for Economic Co-operation and Development
PWD	EU Posting of Workers Directive
SOKA-BAU	Sozialkassen der Bauwirtschaft (collective social fund)
TVG	Tarifvertragsgesetz (collective agreement act)
VDF	Verband der Fleischwirtschaft e.V. (the Meat Industry Association)
Ver.di	Vereinte Dienstleistungsgewerkschaft (United Service Union, Germany)
ZDB	Zentralverband deutsches Baugewerbe (Central Association of the German Building Trade)

WORKERS WITHOUT BORDERS

INTRODUCTION

In 2012, as I was visiting a housing site in Northern Germany, I met a woman named Maria. Maria had moved there from Romania a few months earlier to work in the meat industry. As we got talking, Maria shared with me a concern that is at the heart of this book. "We," she said, referring to posted workers, "are now part of the European Union, but it does not feel like it; we have no representation, no voice, here." She felt excluded because her expectations of a pan-European labor market did not match her actual experiences. She and her colleagues received less pay from the employer than promised in their home countries, worked long or unreliable hours, faced management intimidation, experienced inadequate regulatory oversight, lacked health coverage or the time to attend to medical emergencies, and lived in substandard housing conditions. Maria and her colleagues conceived the European Union (EU) and Germany's place within it to be well regulated. Being part of the European Single Market and constituents of the workforce supporting economic growth and wealth, they equally expected to be protected by the European labor market rights framework. In practice, the workers' experience within the pan-European labor market was rather one characterized by fragility and contingency. As Maria pointed out, she and her colleagues are indeed situated within the European labor market, but many of the rights established within this context are rendered inaccessible to them.

In the European Single Market, labor can move individually via the free movement of labor, or firms can move workers around via the free movement of services. Posted Work is a central feature of employment practices via the freedom of services. Workers are "posted" by their employer to carry out work in one country, usually for a limited period of time, but they remain employed in another country. Workers, so it seems, are without borders. Yet while the reality of a borderless Europe for workers is within reach for many, for a large group of people, this reality seems further away than ever. State borders may have "disappeared." In both theory and practice, the border for the movement of services within the EU is no longer consistent with the edges of the physical territory of the member states. Yet borders still exist. They just exist elsewhere: in unequal pay, in lack of access to collective channels of representation, or in the inability to claim rights. For example, the rebordering process of states intersects with the significant transformations of labor markets in Organisation for Economic Co-operation and Development (OECD) countries since the 1970s. A key change in this process has been the increased flexibility and use of atypical employment contracts such as posted work, substantially altering the organizational activity of the main contracting firm and differentiating between rights of employees working at the main firms and those working at subcontracting firms. This book looks at how workers experience their rights when nation-states have given up large parts of sovereignty over their labor markets, while employed in a precarious employment relationship that stretches across state jurisdictions in the EU.

In theory, posted workers have rights according to the EU Posting of Workers Directive (PWD). Whether this is true in practice, however, is another question. Is a Polish citizen hired by a subcontractor in Cyprus for a job in Germany able to claim the minimum wage? What if the worker was sent from a Bulgarian company to a German meat slaughterhouse? Do EU migrants know which rights are available to them? Can they always access them? How do socioeconomic and cultural factors facilitate or complicate access? The answer to each of these questions is unclear because of limited research on real-world experiences of intra-EU migrants.

This book reports on interviews with and participant observation of posted workers regarding how they experience the posting relationship, the mechanisms that enable access or denial to their rights, their ability to voice concerns over exploitative practices, and their interactions with institutions that should in theory enforce their rights. An actor-centered research strategy helps identify the ways actors make sense of these regulatory processes at the workplace level. This approach can help generate an understanding of the dynamics of change in transnational workspaces in relation to the usage of rules; voice and exit; the possibilities of resistance; and, more generally, how such a pan-European labor market is structured.

Using a bottom-up lens, this book examines how actors interact with institutions (Scharpf 1999) at the workplace level. This book complements the dominant research on EU integration, which is largely based on the belief that individuals act as rational beings and according to the intentions of the policy in question (Kauppi 2010). It considers the actors involved in the posting relationship to do more than produce automatic responses to the regulatory framework but to utilize this framework creatively. By focusing on actor strategies in response to the creation of a pan-European labor market, the book highlights how "actors engage with, interpret, appropriate or ignore the dynamics of European integration" (Woll and Jacquot 2010, 116).

My window to how posted workers experience intra-EU mobility is Germany. This is a country that has traditionally been characterized as having both high labor standards and well-functioning collective representation rights for labor. It has been central to the policy discussion on the PWD. Empirically, a higher number of workers are posted to Germany than to other EU countries (Pacolet and De Wispelaere 2016). Germany also has a history of facilitating the inflow of temporary foreign worker schemes, creating a low-wage work sector. The examination of posted worker experiences takes place in the two sectors where posting is most prevalent: the construction and meat slaughtering industries. The focus on Germany builds on the social science tradition of using changes in the "German model" to theorize broader changes. Germany has always been an important case in the development of the comparative political economy and industrial relations literatures (Unger 2015; Bamber, Lansbury, and Wailes

2011; Hall and Soskice 2001), and building on this tradition enhances the empirical and theoretical relevance of this book. Germany's current role and embeddedness in the European context position it with the potential to again inform the revision of existing theories.

Posted Work, the Nation-State, and European Integration

Just over a century ago, Max Weber addressed the relationship between the nation-state, economic regulation, and seasonal labor at his inaugural lecture in Freiburg. In his politically troubling words, the "swarms of nomads"—that is, Polish seasonal laborers brought in by middlemen in Russia—appeared desirable to employers not only because employers could save on "workers'" dwellings, on taxes to support the poor, and on social obligations, but also because their precarious position as foreigners put them in the landowners' hands (Weber 1994, 9). Yet, he argued, this seasonal labor was preventing unemployed German peasants from reentering employment. The "state's" economic policies, Weber (1994, 9) demanded in a nationalist and discriminatory timbre, ought to rise to the challenge of "defending" the German race and should shut the borders to migration.

More than a century later, the debate is still the same: employers prefer temporary migrant workers as a cheap, exploitable source of labor; agents channel migrants across borders; and, unfortunately, labor migrants are, still today, blamed for rising unemployment and for degrading the nation through "benefit tourism" or "poverty migration." However, the structure in which these developments take place has changed considerably. The Weberian nation-state, able to close the borders of the territory over which it had full authority and employ economic policy as it saw fit, was reconfigured by European integration. The EU has created a single market with reduced regulatory barriers for firms and workers. Part of this labor mobility takes the form of posted work, in which firms based in one EU member state "post" their employees temporarily to another EU member state to fulfill a service.

On the one hand, the PWD defines contractual terms and conditions for posting and establishes that, while posted workers' social insurance and taxes are paid in the sending country, they should receive a minimum wage if it exists in a given industrial sector. On the other hand, posted workers themselves—as well as trade unions, works councilors, labor inspectorates, and the state—are poorly equipped to ensure that these regulatory standards are upheld. This in-between space and the de facto and de jure rights that posted workers hold within this space render them "borderline citizens."[1] To put it differently, while posted workers might be conceptualized as integral to and well regulated within the European and national labor markets at one moment, this could quickly evaporate in the face of certain management practices, a lack of enforcement, exit options being used by employers, and a lack of proper voice options for workers.

Thinking about posted workers as "borderline citizens" points to the contingent, conditional, and even vague place they inhabit within the nation state, as the most contentious issue around the posting regulation was, and still is, the question of which regulatory framework applies to posted workers at their place of work. Polish, Romanian, Portuguese, and Spanish (to name but a few) companies post workers to Germany whose wages and contracts are signed under de facto Polish or Romanian laws, creating islands of foreign law (Hanau 1997) in the territory of the receiving country. Even though the PWD regulates posted workers' inclusion, the structure to claim their rights is still not conclusive. As Cott (1998) noted, "Formal inclusion . . . is never as decisive and determinative as formal exclusion" (1473). The aim of this book is to illuminate and analyze this in-between space and the lives of posted workers within it.

This is not to ignore the considerable research on the free movement of services and posted work. Various studies have investigated the encounters between EU regulation and national labor markets and their highly diverse industrial relations systems, public policies, and legal orders (Kall and Lillie 2017; Cremers 2011; Lillie 2010; Dølvik and Visser 2009; Barnard 2008; Cremers, Dølvik, and Bosch 2007; Eichhorst 2000). These studies discuss how institutions change through the policy process and how power imbalances are created and re-created between the nation state and the EU policymaking body. Other studies have examined how EU member states try to re-regulate their labor markets in light of EU politics toward labor mobility (Alsos and Eldring 2008; Höpner and Schäfer 2007; Dølvik and Eldring 2006; Lefebvre 2006; Menz 2005; Eichhorst 2000). Further, there exist analyses of the tactics of capital and labor in the national re-regulatory processes (Greer, Ciupijus, and Lillie 2013; Refslund 2012; Afonso 2012; Lillie 2010; Krings 2009; Lillie and Greer 2007; Kahmann 2006). Moreover, a vast legal literature has discussed the impact of contentious European Court of Justice (ECJ) rulings on the scope of political economies to regulate their labor markets (Joerges and Rödl 2009; Kilpatrick 2009; Barnard 2008; Davies 2008; Ahlberg, Bruun, and Malmberg 2006).

Scholars have observed that the free movement of services in the form of worker posting has generated a transnational European market for low-skill labor (Dølvik and Visser 2009). Meardi, Martin, and Lozano Riera (2012) noted that worker posting has facilitated "the creation of a hyper-flexible buffer of migrant workers who, being disposable in case of downturn, can carry most of the uncertainty burden without causing political problems" (5). Even though the overall assessment of the free movement of services and worker posting has indeed been negative, we know very little about how posted workers themselves experience the posting relationship (for notable exceptions see Lillie 2010; Berntsen 2016; Danaj and Sippola 2015).

By contrast, this book examines how posted workers and actors involved in the posting relationship actually utilize and experience the European posting framework. Empirically, the book shifts the attention from actors at the policymaking level to those who are the subjects of the matter: transnational posted workers themselves. This distinguishes the book from macro- and national-focused approaches in comparative political economy and industrial relations by zooming in on the *workplace* dynamics in a *transnational* setting. Theoretically, the book draws on adjacent disciplines—industrial relations, comparative political economy, European integration, and migration studies, as well as on discussions on the de-territorialization of the nation state—to magnify their abilities to understand the interplay between changes in work, mobility, and citizenship in contemporary European labor markets.

The issue of posted work lends itself well to this kind of endeavor because, in the posting framework, the regulatory context is to a large extent delinked from insular national territorial regulations. At the same time, the transnational flexibilization of employment relations increases. A central theme of this book is thus the coevolution of changes in territorial political economies and modifications in employment relations through transnational workspaces from the bottom up. The central argument is that national policies are not simply downloaded at the European level (Kauppi 2013), but neither are European and/or national policies transferred as intended by the rule makers to the workplace level. Regulatory dynamics may take different forms throughout multiple levels in the EU. Special attention has to be paid to the embedded and embodied nature of the regulatory framework and the forms of industrial relations structures at the supranational, national, and workplace levels. These levels and the actors at these levels do not exist in isolation to each other but are mutually constitutive of the regulatory space in the EU.

The Regulatory Environment

The context of inclusion and exclusion for posted workers has shifted over time. In the 1960s it was primarily state managed, though in the 1990s and 2000s it became increasingly driven by the autonomous actions of workers and firms (Arnholtz 2013). The market in which posted workers migrate transformed itself from an *international* to a *transnational* labor market. This raises the question of how much posted workers differ from transnational migrants, if at all. They certainly do share certain characteristics. Similarities of posted workers to transnational migrants include being simultaneously embedded in two societies; they settle, to a greater or lesser degree, into the societies of the countries where they work but remain embedded in their home countries at the same time (Glick Schiller, Basch, and Szanton Blanc 1995; Roberts, Frank, and Lozano-Ascencio 1999). However, even though posted workers reside for limited periods in one or multiple countries, their migration process is arranged by their employer, and they often refrain from embedding themselves in countries other than their home country (Çaro et al. 2015). These factors significantly impact the in-between position of posted workers as well as the regulatory spaces they inhabit.

Migrants who migrate and find a job individually must arrange, among other things, a place to live; learn the language and set up financial services; and interact with authorities (Datta 2009; Spencer et al. 2007). The posting relationship is an employer-arranged migration context in the sense that employers mediate posted workers' interactions with host societies. This at once facilitates access to the host society's administrative apparatus and limits interaction with the host society, triggering social segregation. Posted workers have to actively seek out contact with their host-society surroundings.

In general, this means that their lives remain quite disconnected from the host society and region where they temporarily reside. Here, employer-arranged migration reinforces connections with conationals, as posted workers from the same country often share the same work and accommodation environments (Çaro et al. 2015). It also means that the rights of posted workers are increasingly related to their employer instead of the sending or receiving country (Guild 2001). Posted workers, even though they work in the host country's territory, are disconnected to a large extent from the host country's institutional system and labor relations. Language barriers with the host society foster more intensive contact with conationals. For posted workers, foreign language skills are often not a necessity; work teams are oftentimes arranged on the basis of nationality, so, within the workplace, it usually suffices if one member of a workgroup can speak the common workplace language.

The temporary nature of posted work means that migrants are not part of the target group for integration policies in the same way as more permanent migrant groups (Phillips 2010). The rights that posted workers can draw on are part of the regulatory framework of the PWD and its implementation into national laws. The start of the discussion concerning the PWD can be traced to the late 1980s. At that time, the European building unions pleaded for a social clause to guarantee compliance with working conditions and collective agreements in the host country in procurement rules for public works, in line with Convention 94 of the International Labour Organization (ILO) and the Davis-Bacon Act in the United States (Cremers 2009). Despite broad support in the European Parliament, the Council of Ministers reduced the proposal to a voluntary act instead of an obligatory clause. In response, the European Commission introduced a proposal for a directive on the posting of workers in 1991 (Cremers, Dølvik, and Bosch 2007). At the center of the policy struggle has been the question regarding how much the protection of posted workers is on par with the free provision of services (Cremers, Dølvik, and Bosch 2007; Höpner and Schäfer 2012). The PWD was finally adopted in 1996—five years after its first official proposal.

The PWD lays down a bare minimum of employment conditions for workers moving within three posting situations.[2] The underlying condition is an employment relationship between the undertaking making the posting and the posted worker during the period of posting, namely:

1) Posting under a contract concluded between the undertaking making the posting and the party for whom the services are intended
2) Posting to an establishment or an undertaking owned by the group
3) Posting by a temporary employment undertaking to a user undertaking operating in a member state other than that of the undertaking making the posting

Posting to an establishment or an undertaking owned by the group usually involves employees generally being regarded as "expatriates" rather than "posted workers" and is a more common situation for technical and managerial staff (Pedersini 2010). This category of employees often receives a number of benefits for their work abroad. Officially, a posted worker, as defined by the PWD, is a worker who, for a limited period, carries out their work in the territory of a member state other than the state in which they normally work (Directive 96/71/EC). The provision of services is thus only for a limited period of time.

In reality, the "posted worker" classification is often ambiguous. In the best scenario, posted workers are part of a genuine European division of labor between contractors and specialized subcontractors. In the worst scenario, posted workers are bogusly employed as temporary labor. Even though posting does not lead to substandard working conditions per se, it has created an opening for new forms of recruitment that are part of a European market for low-skilled labor in which both the boundaries between mobile labor, posted work, and self-employment are fluid and the line between "temporary" and "permanent" is frequently blurred (Faist 2008). For the sake of clarity, this book thus refers to workers as "posted workers" when they are sent by their employer to work in another country under a service contract. The interviews tried to discern in which country the workers were paying social security contributions as an indication of the posting relationship. In that sense, the term "posted work" is used as a conceptual tool to demarcate the transnational employment relationship and a de facto dependent employment relationship for workers from those moving under the free movement of people. Thus, when referring to posted workers, the particular de facto employment situation is referred to instead of the strict legal definition, which is in itself a legal construction, as multiple rulings by the ECJ have shown.

The Role of the ECJ

Intra-EU mobility has been contentious since its conception. After the six member states signed the Treaty of Rome, Lannes (1956) argued that "a scheme entailing freedom of movement such as that introduced by the Scandinavian countries seems to be out of the question as long as the marked unbalance in the economic structures and social conditions of Western Europe persists" (150). Nevertheless, at the time of conception, workers moved to and from labor markets and welfare states at broadly similar levels of income, and EU regulation ensured that they could secure their social rights in pensions and healthcare. The twenty-eight member states that make up today's EU[3] have very heterogeneous social security provisions, levels of income, systems of public policy and enforcement, and industrial relations practices, not to mention the cultural and language differences among them. This heterogeneity is perceived to result in slow policy negotiations, resulting in minor policy changes over time. By contrast, integration via the ECJ takes less time and can advance more radical decisions because of the absence of political negotiation (Höpner and Schäfer 2012). First and foremost, the ECJ defined posting in such a way that it falls under the free movement of services instead of the free movement of workers. The ECJ regarded posted workers as a "manpower service" and not as labor migrants. Therefore, posted workers are regulated under the free movement of services instead of the free movement of people. The ECJ justified this decision by reasoning that "such a worker [would return] after the completion of the service and [would] not at any time gain access to the labor market of the host state" (Case C-113/89 Rush Portuguesa §15), manifesting the isolated nature of posted workers in the host-country context. Liberal voices welcomed the greater competitive pressure posted work produced that brought an improvement in the allocation of capital (Kahanec 2013). Others, such as trade unions, feared "wage dumping" and the erosion of member states' capacities to regulate their labor markets and social policies.

Moreover, in the cases *Viking*, *Laval*, and *Rüffert*, as well as *Commission vs. Luxembourg*, the ECJ fundamentally reconfigured the posting policy previously agreed on during multilateral negotiations (Scharpf 2008). These decisions have received much attention because they were interpreted as landmark decisions on the struggle between economic freedoms and social regulation in the European common market. In the context of this book, two aspects are important. The first aspect is the reinterpretation of the PWD.

In *Laval*, the ECJ referred to the list in Article 3 (1) as defining the "ceiling" on the "maximum" standards that member states are allowed to impose on posted employees[4] (Kilpatrick 2009, 845–49). With this judicial reinterpretation, the ECJ effectively limited the host countries' room for maneuvering to regulate the labor market. This constraint accelerates races to the bottom in the field of labor standards, a problem that increased as the heterogeneity among member states increased (Scharpf 2006).

The second aspect concerns the restriction on private bodies (such as trade unions) in defending the rights of posted workers. In *Viking* (Case C-438/05) and *Laval* (Case C-341/05), the ECJ ruled that industrial action aimed at representing posted workers from a foreign undertaking could violate the company's freedom to provide services across borders. By ruling as such, the ECJ effectively curtailed trade unions' right to strike (Kilpatrick 2009, 845–49). The PWD and the Services Directive are the outcomes of the EU democratic process. The ECJ has, however, refined the details of posting regulations through judicial integration. This is problematic due to the inherent difficulty in reversing these decisions through the EU democratic process (Höpner and Schäfer 2007).

These decisions have impacted member states' abilities to respond to EU legislation according to national institutional systems. First, the rulings regarded the particular regulatory nature of national industrial relations systems as a constraint on freedom of services (Barnard 2009). This undermines the ability of national industrial relations systems to set collective standards according to their respective traditions, resulting in a "clash of capitalisms" (Höpner and Schäfer 2012; Kilpatrick 2009; Joerges and Rödl 2009). Second, the ECJ intervened in particular national industrial relations institutions, such as the right to strike in Sweden. Third, the cases established that the *minimum* set of rights as set out in the PWD is a *maximum* set of rights, meaning that member states are constrained from enforcing conditions for posted workers beyond the minimum conditions set down in law or in extended collective agreements.

These decisions are important for the context of this book because they constrain member states' abilities to regulate labor markets and protect workers' rights. As a result, posted workers work in regulatory loopholes where companies can draw on different sets of business practices and worker expectations. Lillie and Greer (2007) note that this posted worker isolation can be exploited by firms as a business strategy to shield themselves from national labor regulations and to "isolate migrants from the economic and social norms of the host society" (552). Lillie (2011), drawing on Ong (2006) and Palan (2003), compares this regulatory situation to a "space of exception" (694)—a condition in which the regular law is exempted. However, these spaces still inhabit a particular structure that the following chapters try to illuminate.

Approach and Outline of the Book

This book addresses the complexities of transnational posted work through three key topics. First, it examines how the de-territorialization of national models and employment relations systems opens up exit options for management, enabling it to use the regulatory framework creatively and at a disadvantage for workers. Chapter 2 shows how transnational regulation and de-territorialization impact employment relations in a German case of two industries in which posted workers are most present: the construction and the meat slaughtering industries. Chapter 3 combines institutional theory with strategic perspectives drawn from the sociology of organizations to examine how industrial relations actors "enact" EU rules at the microlevel of the workplace.

Second, it discusses how re-territorialization, or resistance, is possible within these spaces. Chapter 4 shifts the perspective to power and mobilization theory to demonstrate how workers foster community and media support to address contentious workplace issues within the transnational space. Third, the book analyzes the contours of the new structure for employment relations that emerges within the pan-European labor market and its implications for worker voice, regulatory enforcement, and management power. Thus, chapter 5 adopts a more explicitly spatial perspective and looks at how borders are constructed in both regulatory and workplace terms. Chapter 6 summarizes and concludes.

To analyze (1) the implications of the de-territorialization of "bounded" national labor markets, (2) the usage of the regulatory framework and its implications for labor market regulations, (3) the possibilities for resistance within transnational workspaces, and (4) the shifting relationship between the changes in the territorial nation-state and its institutional apparatus and the changes in employment relations in the EU, this book draws on interviews with posted workers from Poland, Romania, Bulgaria, Portugal, and Spain aged between 17 and 53 years working in the construction and meat slaughtering industries in Germany. Interviews were conducted with posted workers, native workers, works councilors, inspectors, and policymakers as well as firms, trade unions, and nongovernmental organizations (NGOs). In total, I conducted 111 interviews with key informants (see Appendix II). Most of this work was carried out over three years between 2011 and 2013, with follow-up interviews occurring in 2014 and 2015 to track more recent developments within the industries.

The book conducts analyses at the firm, industry, country, and EU levels. Such a perspective concentrates on how local actors implement European rules and opportunities (Pasquier and Weisbein 2004) to analyze the evolving balance of power induced by the EU around policy issues (Woll and Jacquot 2010). The approach binding the chapters of this book has been informed by an understanding of the need to link the institutional setting to the actual practices of actors involved to comprehend the full meaning of an institution and its changing nature (Kauppi 2010; Woll and Jacquot 2010; Streeck and Thelen 2005). Concentrating on formal rules when considering political conflict in the EU "would leave some of the most striking features of this transformation in the dark" (Woll and Jacquot 2010, 120). Moreover, the sectoral approach to analyzing power relationships distinguishes this book from macro- and national-focused approaches in comparative political economy literature, providing a multifaceted perspective of political dynamics in transnational workspaces. The following will concisely explicate the main points of discussion relevant for the chapters of this book.

Nation-States and Flexible Management Practices in Transnational Workspaces

Posted work is an example of how European integration restructures relationships between states and actors in ways that challenge the traditional understanding of "nationally organized" economic systems in mainstream comparative political economy. Historically, the formation of borders has had a clear purpose. Territorial demarcation was a necessary prerequisite for the formation of the modern nation-state system. Borders delineated a given territory over which authority was consolidated and order enforced (Weber 1947). Next to a central bureaucracy, citizenship, and the abilities to collect taxes and enforce order, borders were the prerequisite for any state-like formation (Zielonka 2000). The nation-state had a monopoly of control over the movement across the borders of its territory and decisions on who could participate in its labor market (Torpey 1998). Within these borders, each nation-state created a distinct set of institutions that have in turn structured actor behavior. Institutionalist scholars have connected these to national socioeconomic outcomes.

For example, the comparative political economy and industrial relations literatures are inclined to embed actors in nationally bounded sets of relations (Bamber, Lansbury, and Wailes 2011; Hall and Soskice 2001). In these models, institutional complementarities have a tendency to reinforce each other, making a particular set of institutions within different national models resistant to change (Hall and Soskice 2001). With regard to the regulation of posted work, Menz (2005) contends that national varieties of capitalism filter the impact of European regulations. This mediation results in different regulatory outcomes to EU-wide policies for regulating the provision of services. The institutional setup of nationally organized political economies thus influences how EU-level regulation is implemented. This research does not take issue with the view on the potential of national systems to explain the diversity of response to changes in EU regulation; the evidence here underlines the fragility of capital's support for national varieties of capitalism. The aim here is to show that we cannot fully understand EU or national regulation until we connect the way policy is designed and renegotiated with the way actors use it in everyday life and, in this case, in a transnational context.

Like comparative political economy, industrial relations, as a discipline, focuses on national systems as sets of relationships between workplace-based actors within enclosed territorial spaces corresponding to national borders (Lillie and Greer 2007). Research on the dualization of the labor market shows that the parallel circuit of subcontracted workers results in the undercutting of wages, reduction of skill formation, and erosion of union representation (Doellgast and Greer 2007). By its very nature, this industrial relations perspective remains closely tied to the nation-state as a unit of analysis. It does not consider how a worker employed via a subcontracting relationship might collect pieces of protections from more than one nation-state or how nation-states might protect and provide for mobile citizens. Native workers are embedded within the political economy where the work takes place. By contrast, posted workers are legally separated both from the institutional structure of the location of the work and from native workers with whom they share a job site while they are simultaneously alienated from the sending country (Wagner and Lillie 2014).

Moreover, globalization and European integration have started to dissociate, or de-territorialize, the bonds that tied economics, politics, and culture to fixed spatial configurations. Certain rights have been established at the European level for posted workers, but the effects of these rights are ambiguous, since they are established in the absence of "bounded" mechanisms for social solidarity (Wagner and Lillie 2014). This relates to the way internal borders have been removed in the EU integration process. Europeanization can be said to "disembed" markets and detach social relations previously regulated via national social bargains (Höpner and Schäfer 2012) or to "embed neoliberalism," in which market-embedding institutions remain at the national level but are increasingly targeted by supranational liberalization attempts (Van Apeldoorn 2009). European integration opens up exit options for capital but isolates posted workers from collective channels of worker representation. In light of the de-territorializing capacity of posting, specific national re-regulation often remains ineffective at the workplace level. The way in which firms create and exploit transnational workspaces reduces the capabilities of state-centered institutional systems to regulate within their own territories. To understand the evolution of any regulatory institution, it is important to examine the contexts as well as the actions of actors, as they are mutually constitutive (Jackson 2010). Chapter 3 discusses how power imbalances between capital and labor as created at the policy level are translated to the workplace level. The aim of the chapter is twofold: first, to study how firms creatively enact the posting framework and, second, to examine how these mechanisms initiate a process of institutional change through power dynamics at the microlevel, a process generally relevant for theories on institutional change. Findings show that the possibility for firms to diverge from rules is accelerated in a transnational setting due not only to the unequal power dynamics between firms and workers but also to the inability to publicly or collectively enforce rules. The examination of how actors engage with this transnational institution contributes to institutional change theory by bridging the gap between institutional context and its appropriation by firms, posted workers, and unions.

DeCerteau (1984) has pointed out that theory is incomplete without connecting the experience of "everyday life" with the political framework it is embedded in. For example, in his analyses about the politics of the city, DeCerteau (1984) distinguishes between how the "voyeur" and the "walker" perceive the city. While the "voyeur" has an overview of the city from a height, it is one that is distanced from urban activities—the overcrowding and the congestion, the dangers, and the noises; it is a decontextualized and, indeed, illusionary version of the city. DeCerteau (1984) stresses the importance of analyzing phenomena through the view of the "walker" and examining the interactions between those who made the structure and those who use it to create reality. Over the past few decades, the common approach in comparative political economy has been to use the point of view of the voyeur. For instance, discussions that focus on how institutions change have analyzed the change of the design of the institution as opposed to its implementation in everyday life (Hall and Soskice 2001). It is equally important, however, to go beyond the macro economy and assess institutional practices in a more detailed fashion at the individual level (Deeg and Jackson 2007; Jackson 2010). Institutions both constrain and enable action and are dynamic. For example, actors may not conform to the institutional setting if their interests come out of alignment with the expectation and reward structures of the subsystem in which they take part (Greif and Laitin 2004). This becomes problematic when alternative legitimate frameworks present themselves, which actors can access to protect themselves from enforcement.

The posting regulation presents such options to actors. The delinking of labor market regulation from insular national territories creates a space where the regulatory system can be avoided. Firms adhere to the norms on paper but not in practice. This is relevant because the appearance of conformity is often sufficient to attain legitimacy (Oliver 1991). The rule system can be upheld because of the inability of unions and labor inspection authorities to control these gaps. These discrepancies can lead to institutional transformation, even when no sudden shocks or breaking points are prominent (Greif and Laitin 2004). Indeed, Djelic and Quack (2002) have suggested that central foreign actors may become missionaries of institutional change. Beyond simply playing according to their own rules of the game, foreign firms may help institutionalize their rules in new contexts.

Here, national mediation of the European liberalization of services can only partially take place. State-centered border regimes remain foundational elements of the system (Sassen 2005), but their ability to regulate within those borders is limited. Held (1992) usefully distinguishes between "de jure" and "de facto" sovereignty. De facto sovereignty is used in the negative to refer to a loss of authority or control, while de jure sovereignty refers to having supreme power over a given territory. De-territorialization of labor regulation allows for a loss in control over the host-country territory to emerge. This is why it is necessary to examine how actors utilize transnational institutions in these specific situations. The real meaning and function of an institution ultimately emerges only in the course of how it has been interpreted and practically applied by actors (Streeck and Thelen 2005). Delinking territorial contingency with access to political and social protections removes posted workers from the protection they would normally enjoy as regular labor migrants. This provides firms with leeway to creatively exploit regulatory gaps in their cross-border activity. Undermining the nation-state system also undermines the collective goods and stability states provide. Meardi, Martin, and Lozano Riera (2012) discuss the way new labor migrants are in a place of maximum risks and minimum "voice," which is the topic of chapter 4.

Posted Worker Voice and Transnational Action

Trade unions play an ambiguous role in the development of labor market segmentation (Emmenegger et al. 2012; Palier and Thelen 2010). While trade unions have preferred to resist employer pressure toward dualization, they have increasingly concentrated on core members because of a weakening of their position in the social market economy (Palier and Thelen 2010). Therefore, they helped allow for organizational measures and reforms that protect insiders and negatively affect outsiders (Emmenegger et al. 2012). Other researchers have connected increasing market inequalities to the weakening of trade union power. This loss in power impedes effective resistance, resulting in dualization (Benassi and Dorigatti 2015; Korpi 2006). In these accounts, employees' representatives have been much less involved in the labor market liberalization processes (Streeck 2009). Posting is part of the segmentation process because the relationships with labor intermediaries reinforce national/ethnic hierarchies (Refslund and Wagner 2018). In some cases, trade unions have tried to resist employers' segmentation strategies by means of organizing campaigns and collective bargaining targeted to outsiders.

Previous studies have discussed the ability of unions in various host countries to organize migrant workers after the enlargement of the EU in 2004 (Bengtsson 2013; Krings 2009; Fitzgerald and Hardy 2010). Depending on institutional strength, sectoral characteristics, and the ability to innovate (Marino, Roosblad, and Penninx 2017; Baccaro, Hamann, and Turner 2003; Frege and Kelly 2003), unions in, for example, the United Kingdom (UK), Denmark, and Sweden have managed to include migrant workers by employing staff with relevant language skills or by cooperating with other organizations.

Traditionally, German trade unions are known for their political strength within the coordinated market economy embedded in an encompassing institutional framework. However, in certain sectors, there has been a decline in coverage of and a growing inequality within this ideal model. While much of the research on German trade unionism and its institutional position is based on the German metal industry, it is equally interesting and necessary to look at labor-intensive sectors such as construction and meat slaughtering and processing to analyze the position and strategy of trade unions in the context of a pan-European labor market. Moreover, in the context of organizing hypermobile workers, the perspectives of transnational EU posted workers, their own experiences with temporary work, and their everyday practices to cope with the exploitative and uncertain nature of employment have rarely been the subject of attention. This unduly narrows the scope of analysis when trying to comprehend the contemporary contours of power and government in transnational workspaces. While isolation from host-country trade union representation results in the loss of collective voice, workers may use other means to challenge malpractices within transnational workspaces. The various ways they appropriate their rights as EU citizens may differ from traditional channels of voice such as joining unions or voting in union and works council elections.

Given posted workers' predominant exclusion from institutionalized voice channels in the German industrial relations system, chapter 4 explores the conditions for posted worker resistance. As a counterpoint to the literature on institutional stability and change, the chapter traces the process of forming an alliance between the trade union, a community organization, and posted workers and examines the conditions under which it can evolve. The chapter also carves out more explicitly how migrant workers employ strategies to rework (Berntsen 2016) the employment situation to their advantage but do not challenge the structure of the employment relation per se, thereby contributing to the continuation of these employment practices. The case study shows the willingness and need of German trade unions to build coalitions in areas vital to union interests, even though they have traditionally abstained from doing so because of their strong institutional entrenchment. Resistance here is conceptualized as re-territorialization to analyze how workers "disembedded" from the regulatory framework (de-territorialization) can be inserted into an inclusionary framework with collective interest representation (re-territorialization). For the purposes of this book, de-territorialization relates to the disconnect and reconnect of national territory from and to workers in relation to labor market integration. For example, de-territorialization is directly related to the labor process in the example of the Enclosures Acts in England. The act disconnected peasants from grazing land and re-territorialized them onto textiles in the burgeoning garment industry (Elden 2005). In the posting of workers discussion, the term "de-territorialization" was mainly used by legal scholars to denote the decontextualization of labor law and industrial relations systems from particular territorial ties (Mundlak 2009). The concept of territorial embeddedness is used as a tool to further the understanding of industrial relations and labor processes in cases of transnational mobility of both capital and labor. It allows questions of location-bound and non-location-bound actions and the impact of the place on employment relations to be addressed. At the same time, it points to processes of disembedding or de-territorialization of particular importance in this context.

The Political Economy of Borders in the European Labor Market

Borders as lines of demarcation have become so integrated in the way we think that we rarely notice or question them. In light of the various mobility practices in the EU, we have to take a new look at how borders relate to territory, order, and security (Bigo 2013) as well as, indeed, employment relations. Chapter 5 adopts a more explicitly spatial perspective investigating the reconfiguration of borders in a pan-European labor market. Posted work incorporates two trends that have been explored separately in the political science, political economy, and industrial relations literatures. On the one hand, the impact of European integration on the territorial order of modern nation-states is at the heart of a key debate in international relations and comparative politics. On the other hand, the increasing employment of workers via subcontractors or temporary work agencies as a way to weaken labor power and segment the labor force through institutional change dynamics has been explored in the industrial relations and political economy literatures.

The notion of "border" has been the topic of many discussions. Within this book, borders are understood as institutions. They are constructed of demarcating lines that refer to a territorial or functional definition delimiting membership (Bigo 2013). Because of their constitutive nature, borders can give insights into the social ordering of a territory (Hetherington 2003, 64). While political geographers used to think of borders as physical lines on the ground separating one nation-state from another (Minghi 1963), European integration has shown that borders are flexible and constructed by actors (Paasi 1996). Borders can serve and be constructed not only by the state (Berman 2003) but also by transnational companies, diasporas, or other actors (Adamson and Demetriou 2007). Workers, employers, capital, and others—each with their own concerns—construct borders (Herod 1998; McGrath-Champ, Herod, and Rainnie 2010). In a pan-European labor market, state borders shift. Posting via subcontractors and temporary agency firms also shifts the borders of the firm. In fact, Raess and Burgoon (2013) found a positive correlation between EU immigration influences and the incidence of employment flexibility. As labor markets transnationalize, the authority bounded in monolithic concepts of nation-states is disaggregated and various state and nonstate actors are then allowed to claim these competencies, forming new territorial borders.

In the field of migration and mobility, the issue of borders is discussed in relation to how new technologies facilitate controlling the movement of people at the national and external EU borders (Huysmans 2006). For example, Verstraete (2001) provided a vivid account of the involvement of private companies in marketing human detection technologies to the Belgian port of Zeebrugge. This has given rise to an "emerging market in the removal of illegal refugees" (Verstraete 2001, 27). Others have focused on airports as sites where the intersection of technologies, subjectivities, migrations, and markets occurs, giving rise to particular practices of mobility and immobility (Fuller 2003). The discussion on internal EU borders is then particularly geared toward non-EU or illegal labor migrants. Nevertheless, these practices point to the constitutive role of border regimes in giving rise to semipermanent, vulnerable sectors of workers. Borders do not actually prevent the movement of workers but shape the terms under which their movements and subsequent existences take place (Favell and Hansen 2002). In that sense, the EU's border regime can be regarded as a major element in the flexibilization of work (Samers 2003).

Posted work embodies the abolishment of nation-state borders induced by the EU single market. Paradoxically, the nature of the posted workers' regulatory context creates borders within transnational workspaces for workers. These are not as clear-cut as territorial borders but rather disintegrate into a multiplicity of fragmented borders. Borders are not manifested physically but the result of the movement of workers and their interactions with other actors (Guild 2009; Favell 2008). In relation to posting, these borders are very much related to the posting firm. Posted workers do not experience controls on their way to the posting country but at their worksite. Even though the movement across sovereign state borders no longer activates a border for EU citizens, borders still exist in the daily lives of citizens and create a system of "differentiated" memberships for workers.

The reconfiguration of political space lies at the heart of the European project. The new shape of the EU is the subject of manifold studies, but relatively little attention has been paid to the way borders are deconstructed and reconstructed in a pan-European labor market. The assumption seems to be that few borders remain in the single market; however, other researchers have noted that many borders endure (Steen Knudsen 2005). Even though the EU's four freedoms have created a common market without internal borders for labor and services, this book argues that borders have not become obsolete in the context of EU labor market integration. The de- and re-territorialization of state borders intersect with significant changes in labor markets and shifts in the borders of a firm. In developing a framework for understanding the relationship between changes in sovereign borders and changes in employment relations in the EU, chapter 5 draws on European integration literature as well as on comparative institutional analysis and labor geography. It explores the position and creation of borders in a pan-European labor market. It studies the reshaping of the nation-state from the bottom up from the point of view of actors involved in the posting relationship. Findings show the significance of borders to labor market regulation and firm borders to posted workers. This has negative implications for labor rights and transnational solidarity in the EU.

Chapter 1

METHODS AND DATA COLLECTION

This book examines how posted workers and actors involved in the posting relationship engage with the posting framework by investigating four themes:

1) How do posted workers and actors involved in posting interact with the regulatory framework at the workplace level?
2) How does the relationship between national systems of social solidarity and territorial boundedness impact voice and exit incentives for firms?
3) How do posted workers and trade unions protest in poorly regulated workspaces under conditions where traditional avenues to protest are blocked or marginalized?
4) How are borders constructed or reconstructed in a seemingly borderless EU?

Each theme calls for relevant data collection from a broad range of actors. The types of data gathering consisted of the following:

1) Interviews and group conversations with transnational posted workers from various countries, complemented with native worker interviews when possible

2) Interviews with union officials, managers, and works councilors to establish the background facts of particular cases, describe firm strategies, and gather narratives about worker posting and the employment of migrants

3) Interviews with policymakers, employers' association representatives, labor inspectors, political (migrant) activists, and trade union officials involved in policy work to describe legislative and legal struggles taking place around the posting of workers regulation

4) Participant observations of trade union actions and communal posted workers' housing spaces to examine the union's strategies for engaging with posted workers and how posted workers interact among one another

5) Field notes to document certain participant observation activities

The aim was to collect material from actors with opposing viewpoints in order to increase representativeness and to prevent interviewee perspectives and personal viewpoints from having undue influence over the final result so as to achieve a less biased narrative (Stake 1995). Moreover, multiple informants from each category were interviewed. According to Glick et al. (1990), an important advantage of using multiple informants is that the validity of information provided by one informant can be checked against that provided by other informants. Triangulation of the different sources and types of data gathering was used to test the validity of the data (Eisenhardt 1989).

Industry and Workplace Case Study Selection

Industry-level cases are constructed to explore how the specific nature of an industry interrelates with the firm-level cases. The construction and meat industries were selected because of the prevalence of posted workers in those industries. Apart from the quantitative prevalence of posting, the industries have similar structures. Both are structured hierarchically, with a main contractor employing primarily subcontractors for work processes through which vertical disintegration is widely developed. The workplace site locations were determined according to both a media overview and interviews with trade unionists about the whereabouts of large construction sites and meat factories. The determining factors in selecting the workplace case studies were the quantity of posted workers working at the site, its size, and the location (or its accessibility). Size was important because long subcontracting chains are more prevalent at construction megaprojects and in large meat factories.

Firm-level cases are suitable to interrogate the microcosm of interactions between posted workers and actors involved in the posting relationship. They have proved useful in exploring the link between European integration and industrial relations (Marginson and Sisson 2004). The interviews with the actors involved in the posting relationship were organized around these particular worksites. The fieldwork locations ended up being based in Hesse, North Rhine-Westphalia, and Lower Saxony. In addition, I also conducted interviews with relevant actors from other industries and worksites to test validity.

I supplemented these interviews with interviews from other relevant actors. For example, I conducted two interviews with representatives of IG Metall, the dominant German metalworkers' union; two interviews with representatives of the German United Services Trade Union (Vereinte Dienstleistungsgewerkschaft [ver.di]); and one interview with a representative of the German Trade Union Confederation (Deutscher Gewerkschaftsbund [DGB]) to contextualize the developments in the construction and meat industries in relation to other sectors. Moreover, I conducted one interview with a European Commission official from the Directorate-General (DG) for Employment and Social Affairs and two interviews with the EU policy representative of ver.di to trace relevant policy developments in relation to posting. In total, I conducted 111 interviews in various intervals between April 2011 and September 2015.

The semistructured interviews consisted of open-ended questions (Aberbach and Rockmann 2002). Interviews are cited only insofar as doing so does not violate promises of confidentiality and is not likely to result in negative repercussions for the interviewees. The interviews were recorded and transcribed, if possible, and ranged from one to two and a half hours in length. If the interviewee did not consent to the interview being recorded, detailed handwritten notes were taken and were written up at the end of the research day.

Gaining Access to Posted Workers

I made initial contact with posted workers in several ways. "Gatekeepers," for researching German industrial relations, are usually considered to be the trade union and works councilors at the firm level. However, the predominant number of informants from the local trade union offices had no established contact with the posted workforce, or, if they did, they no longer maintained contact because of the workers' site mobility. The same held true for the works councilors. However, they were very helpful informants in selecting the workplace case studies. Moreover, through these initial interviews I established rapport with local union offices, which allowed me to accompany union secretaries on organizing activities or join meetings on how to organize posted workers.

Moreover, community organizations proved fruitful facilitators in establishing contact with posted workers, especially in the meat industry. To secure this cooperation, it was first necessary to meet with gatekeepers several times and provide official information about my status as a researcher as well as information about the study. Conducting interviews at the worksites was not possible, for various reasons. Construction sites and meat factories are highly sealed-off workspaces for which I needed special permission to access. This resulted in management oversight of the interview process, which was likely to skew the answers of the interviewees due to the dependent relationship between posted workers and management. It could have been a strategic choice to conduct workplace-based studies by securing the cooperation of employers. However, I wanted to avoid accessing workers through their employer for reasons such as protecting anonymity and employer retaliation.

Another way of generating initial contact is through participant observation in natural social settings where posted workers congregate (Cornelius 1982). In my fieldwork, I found visiting the workers' housing sites very useful for making initial contact. The trade union or works councilors of the main contractor provided me with the location of the housing sites of workers of various nationalities working at a particular workplace site. For my research purposes, it was important to know which nationalities were working at the site and where the respective nationalities lived, as I needed to hire translators for those site visits. However, difficulties arose because employees are often housed together with a supervisor who controls the private lives of the workers. This complicated initial interaction with the workers, as they worried about management oversight and possible employer retaliation. If anything, this already provided a microcosm of the dependent relationship that exists between employee and employer.

When I was gathering data at the housing sites of the workers, informants were often accessible within a delineated area. This could, for example, be at a housing site where two hundred workers were housed, at which one informant would introduce me to new informants. After making initial contact, I could sometimes use participants' social networks to recruit other participants. In this phase, it was crucial to have a flexible data collection program so that opportunities could be grabbed when they arose, especially in situations when an informant pointed to another informant of relevance during an interview (Goldstein 2002). However, distrust between the workers was also visible at the housing sites. Some were afraid of talking about their situation when other workers were present. Both high labor turnover and management intimidation are possible explanations for the lack of trust between the workers.

Interviews with Transnational Posted Workers

The prime interview focus was to gain insight into how different regulatory systems clashed and the outcomes of these clashes for workers (i.e., how these clashes affect the workers' lives). The exact questions asked and their order depended heavily, among others things, on the interview setting; the legal knowledge of the participant about posting; the quality of the experience of the interviewee being posted; and the trust or social relations established between the interviewee, the interpreter, and the researcher. However, the questions were usually structured into five major sections.

- The first section was intended to collect the personal data of the respondents, including their age group, years of professional and posting experience, nationality, profession, qualifications, and language ability.
- The second section identified the respondents' recruitment channels; the reasons why they wanted to enter posting employment; and the nature of their job tasks, contractual relations, and skill development.

- The third section evaluated the workplace setting, the number of workers at the setting, the nationalities of the workers, impressions regarding interactions among workers at work and between firms, the number of subcontractors, and the supervisory chain.
- The fourth section supported the third section, emphasizing the details regarding working hours, pay, social security contributions, payment methods, bonus payments and deductions, and respondents' impressions about their rights.
- The fifth section was aimed at the respondents' perceptions of their voice options and/or the barriers thereof, beliefs regarding the possibilities of resistance and/or experiences thereof, and knowledge of and opinions on trade unions and works councilors.

I usually finalized the interviews with questions regarding the respondents' future prospects as well as more general questions on social issues or family relations. The workers were aged between seventeen and fifty-three years and originated from Poland, Portugal, Moldova, Spain, Bulgaria, and Romania. The common characteristic of these states at the time of research was that they were all EU member states and had a lower income level and lower social security contributions than Germany (Höpner and Schäfer 2008; Fellini, Ferro, and Fullin 2007). At the time of research, Bulgaria and Romania faced a transition period in Germany toward freedom of movement. The countries fell under the freedom of services in the meat industry but not in the construction industry. To this effect, I encountered more Romanian and Bulgarian workers in the meat sector, while the other nationalities were more strongly represented in the construction sector. Both sectors were male dominated. However, meat packaging and certain parts of the meat slaughtering processes, such as the slicing of the throats of the pigs, were partially performed by female workers. As a result, I conducted five interviews with female posted workers out of the total forty-eight posted worker interviews. The majority (i.e., two-thirds of the interviewees) had previous experience with being posted either to Germany or to a different EU country, while for the minority (i.e., one-third of the interviewees) it was their first time being posted.

Posted workers are in general accommodated together with fellow coworkers, and I therefore often encountered them in group settings. In addition to individual interviews, I consequently conducted group conversations. Interviews were held at the location where interviewees felt most comfortable, a location of their choosing. This differed accordingly; interviews were primarily held either at their housing sites or in public spaces such as cafés or restaurants. Since site mobility of the worker posed a considerable challenge to access, as well as to conduct follow-up interviews, I conducted telephone interviews in instances where interviewees were placed at a distant locale or sent back to their home country. As a result, it was not possible most of the time to trace the evolution of the employment relationship of many of the posted workers; but tracing this was also not part of the design of this research project. Rather, the interviews present a snapshot of a particular social relation and context.

Use of Interpreters

The interviews were conducted in various languages with the help of interpreters who were interviewed before being recruited. Key to the selection process was the interviewers' respect of confidentiality and anonymity as well as the nondisclosure of information about employment relations of any named individual, interpreting experience, and knowledge of and interest in the subject matter. Before the interviews, I trained all interpreters regarding the research objectives, logistics, and access. Information on legal backgrounds and posted worker regulations was provided. As well as participating in training sessions, interpreters were given written guidelines on how to pose questions and probe for answers, how to approach workers, and how to take and write up notes at the end of the research day.

Working with interpreters revealed advantages and disadvantages. Workers were often curious to interact with persons from their country outside their work environment, which helped to establish interest in the interview and trust in a workplace setting hostile toward outsiders, enabling access to posted workers. However, sometimes certain issues, which might seem particularly interesting to other researchers, were not explored in depth by interviewers because the issues were not particularly novel to the interpreter. In that sense, the potential difficulties of using an interpreter, such as the three-way production of data, selective translation, and the reliability of interpretation (Murray and Wynne 2001), are readily acknowledged. Nevertheless, the use of an interpreter was not solely a practical issue but an important approach to ensure that minority voices—in this case, the voices of posted workers from different countries—were heard (Murray and Wynne 2001). Ideally, the interpreter who conducted the interview was responsible for translating the interview from the native language into English or German, depending on the translation capabilities of the interpreter. The translation was discussed at some length with the translators. Throughout this work, the author translated the quotes from German into English, if necessary.

Native Workers

The main focus and the principal time investment of this research was to gain access to and conduct interviews with posted workers. However, if the opportunity arose, I also interviewed native workers who worked alongside posted workers. While this instance occurred in two cases in the meat industry, I did not encounter a native construction worker who worked intensely alongside posted workers. This may have been due to the size of the construction projects I looked at, and I assume this would be different at smaller or medium-sized construction projects. However, the interviews with the works councilors, all of whom had previously worked on construction sites, gave me an in-depth view not only of the historical development of posted work in the industry but also of a native worker's perspective. To test the validity of the data, I triangulated the interview data with primary sources, participant observations, and field notes (Eisenhardt 1989; Yin 2006).

Primary Sources

I examined primary sources such as trade union reports, employers' association reports, and parliamentary questions and government responses to the parliamentary questions to triangulate the collected data. Moreover, I compiled press statements from the trade union, the employers' association, and the government to track legislative processes in relation to posted work. I also collected newspaper articles reporting on the workplace sites. These sources were useful for tracing the history of events and statements made by people in the particular organization that could be used as inputs to the interview questions. Moreover, they helped counteract the biases of the interviews.

Participant Observations and Field Notes

I used interviews as the primary data collection source but complemented those with observations. I used the "observer-as-participant" data collection method (Waddington 1994). In this situation, the researcher maintains only superficial contact with the people being observed but makes no secret of the observation. Participant observation is useful for gaining an understanding of the physical, social, cultural, and economic contexts in which study participants live, as well as the relationships between the people and context (Mack et al. 2005). The visits to the workers' housing sites were very helpful in this regard; they allowed me to observe the relationships between the workers and between workers and management. For example, on some occasions, workers started talking to us only after checking whether all the windows were closed. At other times, after interviewing workers in their apartments, we were told to come back another time but to pretend that we did not know each other so as not to raise suspicion among other workers and management.

In addition, I observed a meeting between the trade union and various NGOs on how to mobilize posted workers, accompanied the trade union in visits to posted workers' housing sites or worksites, partook in a trade union information event for both native and posted workers, joined informal meetings between a community initiative and posted workers, and observed a consultation meeting held at a service center for mobile workers. All these observations gave me the opportunity to validate the data from the interviews and provided insight into the microcosm as to how, for example, the trade union approached posted workers, how they interacted, and how they spoke about the interaction.

Handwritten notes, later converted into computer files, were often the only way to document certain participant observation activities. Moreover, writing and analyzing field notes are an important means of accomplishing an overlap between data collection and analysis (Eisenhardt 1989). Field notes incorporated both observations and analyses separate from one another (Van Maanen 1988). For example, I kept field notes to record my ongoing thoughts throughout the study, including the informal observations.

Analysis

Data analysis consists of "examining, categorizing, testing, or otherwise recombining evidence, to draw empirically based conclusions" (Yin 2006, 126). The analysis for this book was carried out with the help of the computer-assisted qualitative software MAXQDA. This software enables researchers to code and retrieve data and, thus, facilitates the analysis of large chunks of qualitative interview material (Bryman 2001). Coding the interviews helped identify recurrent themes, patterns, and connections (Miles and Huberman 1994). Coding involves marking passages of text that have the same message or are connected in some way to eventually study whether meaningful patterns or differences in the data emerge. In this process, the material from the posted worker interviews was triangulated with expert interviews, union reports, and newspaper articles. Since posted work touches on issues such as labor migration, labor market regulation, industrial relations institutions, territoriality, and the changing nature of the nation state, to name but a few, each chapter required a specific analytical lens and level of analysis through which different themes were explored using the data. The analytical generalization in the study included exploring and developing the concepts and examining the relationships between the constructs. In carrying out this analytical generalization, I acted on Eisenhardt's (1989) recommendation to use a broad range of theories.

One of the main debates in political science today is how institutions within a particular political economy change. In chapter 3, I analyzed the data according to how the posted workers' regulatory framework contributes to an institutional change process within Germany. Many approaches in the literature look for processes of change induced by external market forces. I approached the data by looking at how actors, usually external to the German political economy, induce a process of change endogenously. Throughout my fieldwork it became apparent that actors were operating in two normative systems—one system applied to the host-country rules, but another system was concealed by conforming to the host-country norms and practices only on paper. For this book, I took the construction industry as a level of analysis. More generally, but for chapter 3 in particular, I categorized the data according to different management practices, which were coded as, for example, "deduction for accommodation," "legal on paper," "manipulation of hours and non-payment of minimum wages," and "two contracts." The aim was to extract how firms enact the posting regulation. After several rounds of coding, these codes were grouped under the subcode "semi-compliance," indicating a form of superficial compliance. These findings were similar to observations about institutional change at the policy level, where institutions change due to endogenous rather than exogenous practices. In these instances, change is induced over a long period of time instead of through a pathbreaking shock. Analogous to what Thelen (2004) has called "conversion" and Hacker (2005), in a very different context, has labeled "drift," the coded text segments point to instances in which the institution remains formally intact while policies may change without formal revision, causing ground-level change. While firms officially adhere to the rules, thus leaving them formally intact, they conceal their rule avoidance behind a facade of conformity. By relating my results to similar findings in the institutional change literature, my findings were more generalizable; other researchers produced similar findings in very different contexts (Eisenhardt 1989).

Chapters 3 and 4 are workplace case studies. Workplace case analysis typically involves detailed case study write-ups for each site. While the write-ups involve pure descriptions, they are central to the generation of insight because they help researchers cope with the often-enormous volume of data early in the analysis process (Eisenhardt 1989). The overall idea is to become intimately familiar with each case in order to generalize patterns across cases.

The workplace case study in chapter 4 was chosen because it was a revelatory case. It reflected certain real-life situations of general public interest, and the underlying issues are important in theoretical as well as practical terms (Yin 2006). Chapter 4 contains an analysis of how the appropriation of this regulatory regime impacted collective channels of worker representation. I connected the data to the comparative capitalisms literature, which mainly examines institutional systems within a nationally bounded territory. In my analysis, I connected the institutional characteristics described as "typically" belonging to the German political economy, such as collective voice (trade unions and works councilors) and skill formation, to the de-territorializing effects of European integration and consequent impacts on institutional systems of social solidarity. The key issues in the case study, reflecting the larger trend as identified through interviews at other sites and with different actors, were the posted workers' isolation to the "traditional" collective voice and skill formation characteristics located in the German context.

The posted workers' isolation to the collective voice and skill formation characteristics was coded in several rounds. First, interviews were coded to extract how mobile workers were insulated from skill formation. I created the codes "effect of migration on skill" and "career advancement prospects." Second, the isolation between the union and posted workers was captured by the codes (for trade unions) "access to worksites" and "difficulty of establishing networks onsite." Third, the isolation between the main contractors' works councilors and posted workers was coded under "migrants saying they have no voice," "lack of power," "works council only representing core workers," and "individual voice only via supervisors." Comparing the data with the dominant discussions in the comparative capitalisms literature asks what the findings are similar to, what they contradict, and why (Eisenhardt 1989). While the case study revealed that the institutional characteristics labeled as typical for the German model are still in place, it also showed that they did not apply for posted workers. This is similar to dualization tendencies in the German labor market, but in this instance, accessing different institutional systems was used to isolate workers instead of gaming the German labor market regime itself. Codes representing this relationship were assembled under the subcodes "extraterritorial" and "territorial practices."

The workplace case study found in chapter 4 is useful because the case revealed a process uncommon to the German system of industrial relations: trade union coalition-building with community organizations. The codes used to disentangle how the cooperation between the union, the community initiative, and the posted workers was established and sustained were, for example, "community initiatives/mobilization," "workers taking actions on their own behalf without the union," and "non–union-related mobilizations." From the coded data, I was able to build abstractions and connect these to theoretical concepts and theories (Merriam 1988).

Chapter 5 identifies key problems between labor mobility and EU labor market integration. While the literature on European integration and the territorial structuring of politics examines the current shape of the EU and its borders (Del Sarto 2013; Kostadinova 2013), deeper debates on the conceptual understandings of how the debordering of a political territorial space affects the European labor market and its mobile workers are only beginning (Meardi 2012). Chapter 5 takes this research further by searching for the position and the creation of borders in a seemingly borderless European labor market. I analyzed the data according to patterns of functional and symbolic borders—the lines trade unions draw when they talk about posted workers, the lines firms draw in their hiring or subcontracting process, and the state lines that emerge for public administration officials in relation to worker posting. Codes that reflected the administrative borders for labor inspectorates based in two member states were "difficulty inspecting foreign contracts and firms," "difficulties between labor inspectorates," and "limited mandate of control labor inspectorates." The information on borders drawn between firms in the posting relationship was reflected in the codes "labor market segmentation by firm due to position in the contracting chain" and "difference between subcontractor and main contractor." Two types of borders emerged from the data: (1) firm borders that separate workers from the host-country institutional industrial relations systems and (2) borders for labor market regulation that inhibit the enforcement of labor rights. These borders have a significant impact on the way trade unions can effectively interact with posted workers, inhibiting the creation of social solidarity across borders. These findings were used to create a bottom-up analysis to investigate of the reshaping of the nation state (Radaelli and Pasquier 2006).

Chapter 2

Posted Work and Transnational Workspaces in Germany

A manager of a German slaughterhouse, dressed in proper, white hygienic clothes and donning a hairnet, steered me through the big hallway of the large slaughtering complex. Pristine white tiles covered the floor. The distinct smell of slaughtered meat and the chilled air of the cooling chambers were omnipresent. I had come to one of the four largest slaughterhouses in Germany, with an annual turnover in 2015 of approximately eight million processed pigs. In 2015, five thousand of the slaughterhouse's workers were core employees, while over 50 percent of the workers were employed via temporary agency contracts or via subcontractors. "Outsourcing has existed for a long time already," the manager told me. "But the company started to use subcontractors extensively at the end of the nineties because it was more competitive that way" (interview with management, 2012). It was during that time, when outsourcing first started becoming a normal practice, that Monika, a worker at the same firm whom I talked to at a later stage, worked in the slaughterhouses. She was working the night shift when demand rose significantly for cured ham for the Christmas period. Management wanted the workers to work even longer hours and on Sundays but was not prepared to pay them accordingly (interview with native workers, 2012). The workers demanded more pay for the additional hours, but, in retaliation, management started to phase in subcontractors for the periods in which additional market demand occurred. These subcontractors had their home bases in countries such as Poland, Romania, and Hungary, countries that began to post workers on temporary contracts to German slaughterhouses.

In the construction sector, the usage of subcontractors also significantly increased during the 1990s. From 1990 to 1995, the German economy experienced a construction boom owing to a stimulus from unification and related construction projects in East Germany, including the decision to move the capital to Berlin (Menz 2005). During this period, larger companies began to act as general contractors and outsourced more specialized tasks to national subcontractors (Rußig 1996). By the mid-1990s, the construction sector experienced a crisis. The influx of posted workers from lower-wage countries caused a downward spiral in bidding for both public and private jobs (Menz 2001). As a consequence, between 1995 and 2010, 50 percent of native construction workers were replaced with workers employed at foreign service firms (Bosch, Weinkopf, and Worthmann 2011). One construction worker recalled that subcontractors were initially used in a similar fashion as in the meat industry to cover peak demand, but today subcontractors are always employed on construction sites (interview with native construction worker, 2012). According to him, "With subcontractors, one can make more money because the pay and salary is lower than here in Germany. So, there is already a range of 1:3 in the salary levels. This is the meaning and purpose of the whole subcontractor, and the bad thing is that, then, also, the people are actually satisfied, because they have no work at home at all. There is such a wandering movement, and they are driven out of their country practically because there are already people who are cheaper. So, it's not about pay, but just about survival" (interview with native construction worker, 2012).

The story of posted work is in many respects intertwined with the realities of subcontracting within the national labor market. Theoretically and empirically, posting relates to the trend to outsource production vertically, thereby segmenting the labor market, reducing voice options for workers, and increasing exit options for employees (Keune 2015; Hassel 2014; Brinkmann and Nachtwey 2013; Emmenegger et al. 2012; Kalleberg 2001; Jaehrling and Méhaut 2012; Bosch and Weinkopf 2008). However, this book argues that it adds yet another dimension to the empirical and theoretical knowledge of labor market dualization—namely, the transnational scope. The aim of this chapter is to examine how Europeanization opened up exit options for capital and constrained (and continues to constrain) the rights of unions, works councils, and mobile workers, thereby creating a transnational "in-between" or "borderline" space that allows for the importation of informal work practices, which places these imported workers into "regime competition" (Streeck 1992) side by side with the German employment relations system. Regime competition occurs between national economies and between work groups of workers who may be next to each other at a worksite, employed by different firms to signify the different national regimes (Streeck 1992). In this way, nationally bounded firm strategies of labor market dualization interact with and reinforce segmentation via transnational subcontracting, significantly impacting the availability of voice mechanisms for workers in the German political economy.

This chapter examines the opening of this territorially bounded space in the context of labor market dualization in the German political economy in a threefold manner: (1) it relates the literature on labor market dualization to the changes in the nature and organization of the Westphalian state system—that is, in the ways in which state regulatory authority is connected not so much to national territorial boundaries but to the trend to outsource production vertically; (2) it contextualizes the movements of posted work, as far as possible, within the EU and to Germany in the context of the European Single Market; and (3) it discusses policy changes in the German political economy and in the two sectors of this book, construction and meat, against the background of the respective industrial relations systems. Findings of the chapter show that declining territorial boundedness allows firms to circumvent key German industrial relations institutions. Deterritorialization of regulation is likely to lead to a decline in the cohesion of national systems in general, particularly in systems that are institutionally dense and rely on collective voice.

Opening the Borders of the German Model

A territorially demarcated space, such as the state, offers a framework within which common norms are formulated and established. Solidarity, it has been argued, is primarily valued because it offers the possibility for a group to articulate and is effective within a homogenous, demarcated space (Hoffmann 2006). Rokkan (1999), drawing on Hirschman's (1970) concepts of "exit" and "voice," explained how the scope of economic actors to pursue their interests was defined by territorialization. The establishment of borders was instrumental in establishing an institutional "voice" for those within them and discouraging exit. For example, collective bargaining, just like labor market regulation, was territorialized by embedding a legal pattern within and through the state, because its coverage was usually limited to employers and workers within the territory's borders (Mundlak 2009). Territorial boundedness and coherence were thus requirements for the efficient functioning of industrial relations institutions.

The industrial relations institutions of collective bargaining and works council worker representation still exist at the German national level. However, they seem to be, in the words of Busemeyer and Trampusch (2013), "exhausted": they still exist but are not effective with regard to certain groups of workers, such as posted workers. Trade unions struggle to include posted workers in collective channels of representation, and works councils are legally constrained from interacting with this workforce. Europeanization can be regarded as an opening up of exit options. It is a threat to territorially bounded, collective solutions insofar as it challenges the territorial control of nation-states. Firms can exit from the industrial relations system without having to actually exit the geographic territory. In the short term, this may result in hybrid solutions. In the longer term, we may witness a decline in the provision of collective goods.

These re-regulatory dynamics coevolve alongside similar, or complementary, labor market segmentation approaches within states as unified entities. The "German model" still covers a significant proportion of workers. However, a complex labor market of low-wage workers outside that system has grown (Bosch and Weinkopf 2008; Palier and Thelen 2010; Thelen 2009). The so-called Hartz reform package, implemented by the red-green government in 2003, together with the controversial Agenda 2010 reforms of the labor market, paved the way for a paradigm shift in the German labor market and social policies. Among other re-regulatory measures, Minijobs, a form of marginal employment that is generally characterized as part-time with a low wage, was expanded, atypical employment was liberalized, the age threshold for the application of repeated fixed-term contracts was lowered, start-up (e.g., "Me Inc.") subsidies were expanded, and the master craftsman's diploma as required in many crafts was abolished (Menz 2010; Eichhorst and Kaiser 2006).

As a consequence, unions and collective bargaining institutions have become less encompassing (Cremers, Dølvik, and Bosch 2007). Instead of decommodifying labor, collective agreements are now used to introduce competition within the company's workforce, creating "core" and "peripheral" workforces (Holst 2014). Dual labor markets can be seen as an attempt to continue to access the collective goods provided by the organized economy while creating less organized workspaces walled off from the organized economy in various ways. Labor market segmentation scholars have pointed out that, with regard to migrant workers, the primary labor market is usually reserved for native employees, whereas migrant workers are situated at the bottom of the labor market (Piore 1979; Bonacich 1972). The former is made up of stable employment relationships with worker protection, whereas the latter is insecure and serves to buffer the business cycle.

Posted work is thus likely to produce labor market segmentation similar to vertical disintegration for native and other groups of migrant workers. The result is a decrease in collective goods and an increase in exit. Rather than being fundamentally different, these processes are both part of and signal the variegated nature of regulatory configurations in European political economies (Brenner, Peck, and Theodore 2010). However, labor mobility in the EU occurs in a space that blurs the distinction between "national" and "international" (Guild 2009). Not only do the sending or receiving countries shape the rights of workers; the interaction between those frameworks that are embedded *within* the European supranational policy framework shape transnational workspaces.

Transnational workspaces—in this case, on large construction sites or in large slaughterhouses—redefine the meaning of host-country employment relations. Even though labor market dualization has become part of the fabric of the German political economy, the widening and deepening of the Single European Market adds a different layer to dualization in terms of reconfiguring the space in which work occurs, how it can be regulated, and how workers' voices are to be exercised.

A fundamental characteristic of the modern nation-state and of democratic societies is the territorial basis of their legislation (Supiot 2009). The territorial principle also extensively regulates industrial relations and working and employment conditions. Most supranational regulations concerning employment conditions leave this basis in place. For example, when labor migrants cross borders via the free movement of persons, they enter a new legal system and become subject to the legislation of the destination country. By contrast, posted workers move as dependents of service providers. As a result, their employment relationship is embedded in (at least) two national contexts, and social security contributions are paid in the home country. Even though they work in the territory of the host country, they fall under a different regulatory framework and are largely excluded from the host-country institutional system. One difference is that the labor rights of posted workers are more limited than those of migrants individually working in another EU member state. While migrant workers are regulated under an *international* framework, posting follows a *transnational* pattern because the employment relationship is mediated by the employer of the posted workers instead of by the host country (Lillie 2011). While the posting regulation has existed for decades, it took on a new dimension with the Eastern European enlargement.

Labor Mobility in the Pan-European Labor Market

The establishment of minimum conditions for workers has for many years been considered a landmark in the European trade union movement's attempt to influence EU legislation. While, initially, the PWD had little impact because of a decline in posting in the late 1990s, the issue regained importance with the accession of ten Eastern European and Mediterranean island countries to the EU by 2007.[1] However, as of right now, it is difficult to accurately estimate the quantitative importance of posted work. The portable document A1 is currently the only register of information on posting data (Cremers 2011). Employers posting workers to an EU member state are required to apply to the relevant national authorities for an A1 document. The document exempts workers from paying social security contributions in the country where they are temporarily working and proves they do so in their county of residence (Council Regulations 1408/71 and 574/72).

The European Commission estimated that, in 2011, a total of 1.51 million A1 documents were recorded across the EU-27 and Iceland, Liechtenstein, and Norway (European Commission 2012). In comparison with data from 2010 (1.33 million) and 2009 (1.27 million), there was a strong and continual increase in posting. In 2011, around 60 percent of all postings (compared with 63 percent in 2010) originated in the EU member states that joined the EU before 2004 and almost 40 percent (compared with 37 percent in 2010) in the EU-12 member states that joined in 2004 and 2007. Postings originating in European Economic Area (EEA)–European Free Trade Association (EFTA) countries accounted for only 0.2 percent of all postings (European Commission 2012).

The main sending countries of posted workers in 2011 were Poland, Germany, and France, followed by Romania, Hungary, Belgium, and Portugal. Germany and France were the main receiving countries, followed by the Netherlands, Belgium, Spain, Italy, and Austria. According to the European Commission's (2012) data, workers posted from the Czech Republic, Hungary, Poland, Slovakia, Slovenia, Romania, and Bulgaria were primarily sent to Germany. The secondary destinations of posted workers from these countries were France, Belgium, the Netherlands, Austria, and Italy. A main destination for posted workers from Estonia was Finland, while workers from Latvia posted to Germany and Sweden. Posted workers coming from Lithuania mainly went to Norway, Germany, and France (European Commission 2012). Between 2010 and 2011, the A1 data indicated that the number of posted workers sent abroad increased the most in relative terms (more than a 70 percent increase) from Slovenia, Romania, Latvia, Estonia, Lithuania, and Bulgaria. In absolute terms, the number of posted workers sent abroad from Germany, Poland, Hungary, and Slovakia also strongly increased. On the contrary, the number of workers posted to Spain and Greece decreased, most probably in relation to the decline of labor demand subsequent to the financial crises in these two countries (European Commission 2012).

Some EU member states do not produce figures by economic activity, including Germany and France, two countries with a large number of postings. The European Commission data on A1 documents stated that, for fourteen countries, on average, around 43 percent of A1 documents issued were for the construction sector. Around 27 percent of the A1 documents were issued for activities in the service sector (European Commission 2012).

Nevertheless, the available data provide only the number of A1 certificates issued in each country. They do not contain any information on the duration of postings or the hours worked. Therefore, the present data are not an indicator for labor input. Moreover, a structural analysis of the labor market impact of postings is prevented by the lack of sectoral breakdowns for the data of the main sending countries and a general lack of detail by economic activity. While postings tend to concentrate on a few specific activities (e.g., construction), the available data are not detailed enough to allow any deeper analysis (European Commission 2012).

In addition, there is still some uncertainty as to what extent the numbers of A1 documents recorded by countries are a precise proxy of the actual number of postings taking place (Mussche, Corluy, and Marx 2017). First, the number of certificates can include duplications. An employer can request more than one A1 form for an employee if the employee is posted to different countries within a year. Thus, the number of postings is not necessarily equal to the number of posted persons. Second, the certificates do not distinguish between different types of postings. For example, any monitoring of posted workers will likely include expatriates in the overall numbers. To get an accurate picture of the number of posted workers, it would be necessary to discriminate between posting via a subcontractor, via a temporary work agency, or within companies. Third, many employers do not comply with the requirement to apply for the certificate for their employees. The A1 forms are thus likely to underestimate the overall number of posted workers. Fourth, national data are available in only a limited number of countries. The available data are noncomparable across countries because they are collected according to different criteria and purposes. For example, while the Belgium LIMOSA system is based on the national mandatory register system, France collects data via the French labor inspectorate. The German system is limited to the construction sector, and the Danish RUT-register is equally not comprehensive regarding content and coverage (Ismeri Europa 2012). In general, the numbers found on the basis of these social security forms are considered to represent the absolute minimum amount of posting (IDEA Consult and ECORYS Netherlands 2011).

In Germany in particular, over the past ten years, immigration from other EU countries has increased significantly. A government report identified socioeconomic differences, the downturn in Southern European countries, and Germany's low unemployment rate as key factors in increased immigration from Romania, Bulgaria, Estonia, Latvia, Lithuania, Poland, the Czech Republic, Slovakia, Slovenia, and the southern EU countries as well (Expert Council on Integration and Migration Annual Report—SVR

2013: 58). The figures for these countries have increased as much as fivefold, from 35,131 arrivals in 2004 to 180,733 in 2012. The number of arrivals from Austria, Belgium, Denmark, Finland, France, Germany, Greece, Ireland, Italy, Luxembourg, the Netherlands, Portugal, Spain, and Sweden has increased by 74.9 percent, due primarily to increased migration to Germany from the southern EU countries since 2010 (SVR 2013, 57–58).

Overall, migrant workers are at a disadvantage in the labor market (Engels et al. 2012). The disadvantages are most pronounced in the case of non-EU immigrants, but figures for citizens from the new member states also show higher unemployment rates and more precarious working conditions in the forms of temporary jobs, part-time work, and self-employment compared with the German population. The less favorable labor market situation for migrants is reflected in their income levels. In 2009, net monthly income was below €900 in 18 percent of households in which the main breadwinner was from an immigrant background. Only 13 percent of such households had a net monthly income over €3,200 (WZB Datenreport 2011). The number of foreign citizens on low wages has risen by 2.8 percent from 2010 to 2014, while the percentage of low-paid workers with German citizenship fell by 1.5 percent over the same time span. Similarly, the unemployment figures for 2013 show that the percentage of workers with foreign citizenship was 15.4 percent but was only 6.75 percent for German citizens. In January 2013, unemployment among foreign citizens rose by 6 percent compared with the previous month, while among workers with German citizenship it rose by just 0.9 percent. This may have been an indication of discriminatory practices toward migrant workers during a downturn (Lindemann 2013).

Statistics show that EU migrants are overrepresented in precarious forms of subcontracted work, especially in the construction and pig slaughtering sections. Legal obscurities and loopholes in existing frameworks on intra-EU mobility have created a complex system in which firms employ posted workers or migrant workers via temporary agencies to reduce labor costs and in which migrant workers face varying degrees of substandard employment conditions (Cremers 2011). Migrants are likely to be employees of temporary work agencies, and this likelihood is three times greater if they are non-German citizens (Federal Statistical Office 2014). In many cases, employment as a temporary agency worker has a negative effect on migrant workers' employment conditions and length of employment. Even though the

Temporary Employment Act establishes the right to equal pay and equal treatment for temporary agency workers from the first day of an assignment at a user-company (this has been the case since 2003), the law still allows for exemptions from this principle provided they are stipulated in a collective agreement, which is generally the case (Weinkopf, Hieming, and Mesaros 2009). Moreover, temporary agency workers face a number of risks: they often work in difficult work situations; receive disproportionately low wages; and have reduced employment security, substandard access to further training, and lower job satisfaction (Artus 2014; Vogel 2004; Brehmer and Seifert 2007). The same is true for posted workers working for foreign-based subcontractors except that they are regulated via the posting framework, which disembeds this workforce from the national system wholesale instead of carving out a different regulatory regime within the system. A former construction worker remembered the 1960s and 1970s, when the so-called guest workers were integrated into the preexisting structures of the firm, which also had works councilors. However, today, migrant workers are not integrated into preexisting structures of the firm. They work in teams separate from the core workers. "The separation is institutionalized," he said (interview with native construction worker, 2011).

The German Regulatory Framework for the Posting of Workers

The trend of outsourcing production was already in process when the borders of Eastern Europe were beginning to open (Wilpert 1998). But this trend was molded further into the fabric of the labor market when the German government decided to launch several new temporary migrant worker programs in the 1990s. These programs were not on the same scale as the post–World War II guest worker programs (Wehler 2008). However, they were significant in the sense that, being temporary, they created a set of structural conditions that determined how the new migrants were to be integrated into the labor market. In the 1990s, Germany issued a total of three million project-related and seasonal work permits (Bundesamt für Migration und Flüchtlinge 2010). As Ellermann (2015) argued, the policymakers wanted to ensure that the temporary nature of migrant work under the new arrangements would remain temporary, unlike their counterparts in the earlier "guest worker" programs. Some have argued that Germany, as the paradigmatic guest worker state, continues to be "haunted by the mistakes, failures, and unforeseen consequences of the guest worker era" (Freeman 1995, 890). Originally intended to fill temporary labor shortages, the guest worker system resulted in the permanent settlement of large numbers of migrant workers, which transformed Germany into an ethnically diverse country of immigration (Ellermann 2015). The establishment of the free movement of labor and provision of services within the EU opened the borders to all citizens of EU member states and started a new wave of migration. This too was characterized by temporary work arrangements for EU citizens in the forms of posting and temporary agency work, creating a dual labor market.

In 1996, Germany adopted the German Posting of Workers Act, at the same time that the EU PWD (Directive 96/71/EC) was passed, which was transposed into German law in 1998. A particularity of the German Posting Law (according to §2) is its limitation to certain sectors instead of encompassing the whole national economy. Sectors have to be included individually in the law. While the construction sector was the first included sector, the meat industry was the most recent addition at the time of writing. The law initially included the construction, building, cleaning, and mail services industries and was amended in 2009 when six other industries were included: the care sector (elderly care and ambulant treatment), security services, waste management (including street cleaning and winter services), training and educational services after the Second or Third Book of the Social Code, laundry services in customer business objects, and special mining work in coal mines. Within these branches, posting firms have to respect the *lex locis laboris* and pay posted workers according to the collective bargaining agreement of the sector. Workers employed in sectors not included in the law can be paid according to the country-of-origin wages. This was the case for the German meat industry until 2014 (as will be elaborated on later).

The German Posting of Workers Act defines contractual terms and conditions for posting in the framework of the A1 document (formerly E101 forms) and lays down that, while posted workers' social security contributions and taxes are paid in the sending country, workers should receive a minimum wage if it exists in a given industrial sector. Finally, the act introduced the concept of joint liability (§14), whereby a German company that signs a service contract with a foreign subcontractor becomes liable for the compliance of the binding working conditions for these workers. This legal aspect, also known as chain liability, is particularly useful in cases of pay dumping or illicit employment within the host country (Houwerzijl, Peters, and Jorens 2012). The lack of enforcement of this liability, however, is particularly striking due to the gray zone that develops down the subcontracting chains (Bogoeski 2017), as will be shown in the later chapters of this book.

With the advent of Eastern European accession, Germany, alongside Austria, applied a transitional period to the free movement of services insofar as workers worked in the construction sector, namely, in building maintenance and/or interior design (Donders and Sengers 2009). This exception did not apply to the meat sector. In 2007, Germany again made use of the transitional arrangements on the freedom of services in relation to Bulgaria and Romania joining the EU in the construction but not the meat industry (until December 31, 2013) (Kahanec, Zaiceva, and Zimmermann 2010). The trade unions in Germany were involved in lobbying for transitional arrangements after the 2004 enlargement and, thus, actively opposed the free movement of labor within the EU, citing concern to protect the national labor market from social dumping (Cremers 2011; Meardi 2012). While Krings (2009) stressed that this union policy should be viewed as a concern over the preservation of labor standards instead of viewing it as "anti-immigration" (56), others have underlined the risk of conflicts between eastern and western trade unions due to their diverging interests during the accession process (Meardi 2012; Galgóczi, Leschke, and Watt 2009). The policy shows that the frame of reference for trade unions remains the national one despite declarations of international solidarity (Marino 2015). This is important in the context of this book because it highlights the bordering tendencies between national established collectives, transnational migration, and the in-between space in which posting takes place.

Domestically, the trade unions in the construction and meat sectors concentrated their efforts on establishing a lowest wage floor. Important to note is the absence of the statutory minimum wage in Germany until January 1, 2015. The lack of the statutory minimum wage significantly influenced the wage negotiations in the construction sector to ensure a low wage ceiling for posted workers. It equally influenced the structural conditions in the meat industry, the latter of which was out of the scope of the Posting Law until 2015, meaning that the sending country wages were applicable because of the absence of a generally binding sectoral minimum wage. Before 2015, in sectors that were not specified in the Posting Law, posted workers could legally receive the minimum pay of their sending countries. Legal exceptions, through the country-of-origin principle, are an important factor in keeping posted migrants separate, but equally relevant are industrial relations practices and internal organizational practices that firms carry with them, as will be explained in the following chapters. However, the opening of the European space has placed the traditional collective bargaining and collective employer-employee relationship in the German setting under enormous pressure. Cross-border recruitment and employment in nonstandard and often precarious forms of work in sectors where trade unions' power has decreased since the 1990s (such as in construction and meat processing) has increased the bargaining position of employers over trade unions. Moreover, temporary cross-border movements further exacerbate the decline in union power and the importance of nation-state frameworks for collective worker organization and representation. The loss in union bargaining power, the usage of exit options of employers, the impact of the transnational market, and the creation of a separate labor market with distinct wages and working conditions facilitated through ambiguous subcontracting are all reflected in the policy frameworks and their developments in both the construction and the meat sectors.

Posted Work in the German Construction Sector

The construction industry is one of the most important sectors in Germany. The construction companies in the German construction industry generated sales of €101.1 billion in 2014 (Federal Statistical Office [Statistisches Bundesamt] 2016a, 2016b). This was the first time that the value of €98.8 billion from 2000 was exceeded. In general, sales have continued to grow since 2009. This has mainly been due to housing construction, which has benefited from low mortgage rates. With increasing size, the construction companies are producing an ever-smaller part of the construction output themselves and are increasingly active as general contractors that hand over a large part of the construction output to subcontractors (Bosch, Weinkopf, and Worthmann 2011). In 2012, the share of subcontractors in the gross value of production totaled almost 30 percent (Hauptverband der deutschen Bauindustrie 2015). The number of employees in the construction industry has continually declined since 2000 (Federal Statistical Office

2016b). As with employees, the number of enterprises in the construction industry has also been declining. At the beginning of the 2000s, more than 80,000 construction companies were active in Germany. In 2015, there were still 73,664 active enterprises (Federal Statistical Office 2016b). Small and medium-sized craftsmen predominantly characterize the construction sector. Almost three-quarters of all construction companies have fewer than ten employees. On the other hand, larger firms with more than fifty employees tend to be the exception and represent just 3 percent of all construction companies.

Workers in the construction industry in Germany are represented by the industrial union Bauen-Agrar-Umwelt (IG BAU), which was established at the end of 1995 by a merger between the Bau-Steine-Erden industrial union and the horticulture, agriculture, and forestry trade union (Bosch and Zühlke-Robinet 2003). The union consists of the central federal organization, which is divided into thirteen national associations and ensuing associations. Due to shrinking membership figures, IG BAU in 2015 was the fifth-largest DGB single union with some 273,000 members. In 1996, the year the union was founded, there were 700,000 members, but already in 2000 there were only 540,000 members (Deutscher Gewerkschaftsbund 2016). The collective bargaining treaties negotiated centrally for the entire federal territory alone are the responsibility of the federal executive committee for collective bargaining.

On the employer side, two umbrella organizations at the federal level are responsible for the representation of interests and collective bargaining. These organizations differ in their structure and the companies they represent. The Central Association of the German Construction Industry (Zentralverband deutsches Baugewerbe [ZDB]) represents the interests of mostly small and medium-sized craft enterprises in the construction industry. According to its own data, 35 member associations are represented, which are divided into regional associations as well as regional handicrafts. In total, the ZDB represents about 35,000 member companies with approximately 250,000 commercial employees, 50,000 employees, and 20,000 trainees. The main Association of the German Construction Industry (Hauptverband Deutsche Bauindustrie [HDB]) is the umbrella organization of 15 national associations of employers in the construction industry and represents the interests of the mostly larger construction companies with at least 20 employees. According to its own data, about 2,000 companies are members of the

HDB, which together employ about 100,000 commercial workers, 50,000 employees, and 5,000 trainees.

The structure of both employers' associations can be referred to as the "association of associations" (Bosch, Weinkopf, and Worthmann 2011, 34). The regional associations are largely self-employed, can leave the umbrella organizations at any time, and abolish the right of collective bargaining to the umbrella organizations (Bosch and Zühlke-Robinet 2003). The only exceptions are the wage and salary wage agreements of the construction industry, which are negotiated by industrial associations. However, they have a significant influence on the content of the negotiating instrument and must be satisfied by acceptable tariff results. The challenge for the umbrella organizations is to coordinate the heterogeneous members' interests to reach a consensus on collective bargaining.

The most important regulatory content in the context of worker posting was and is the negotiation of the lowest wage bracket, which served as a wage floor before the introduction of the statutory minimum wage. In 1996, when the German Posting of Workers was implemented, it could not refer to a statutory minimum wage or to de facto universally binding collective wage agreements (Eichhorst 2005). To conform to European law, a minimum wage had to be negotiated between the social partners in the construction industry. It then had to be declared universally binding by the corresponding federal minister. According to §5 of the collective agreement act (Tarifvertragsgesetz [TVG]) at the time, collective agreements could be declared generally binding by the federal minister of labor if one of the parties to the agreement so requests, if at least half of the workforce is already covered by the collective agreement, and if there is a public interest in the general applicability of the collective agreement and an equal number of representatives of the umbrella organizations of employers and trade unions that form the tariff committee that agree to the general applicability.

The social partners had to agree on the universal applicability of this wage regulation to all companies in Germany before the law could take effect. Both sides had three votes in the relevant Ministry of Labor's commission on wages. In this case, the Confederation of German Employers' Association (Bundesvereinigung der Deutschen Arbeitgeberverbände [BDA]) refused to accept universal applicability (Eichhorst 2000) until the wage bracket was significantly lowered. The union thus accepted a lowest wage level significantly lower than the already-existing lowest wage bracket within the collective bargaining agreement. The outcome has left ample room for employers to use transnational subcontracting to "exit" from higher wage brackets in the collective bargaining agreement.

Posted Work in the German Meat Sector

Cases of violations of labor conditions have emerged in major German meat processing companies over the years. Exploitative working conditions have reached national as well as international attention. Domestically, these practices have been deplored as modern slavery (Doelfs 2012), while French workers took to the streets to protest against social dumping practices in the German meat industry because they put French jobs in jeopardy (Blume 2013). At the EU level, the Belgian government lodged a complaint with the European Commission against abusive posting practices in Germany, arguing that it created unfair competition and undermined the Belgian industry. According to the complaint, "shameful practices" were found, especially in the meat processing sector, the majority of whose workers are posted via employment agencies mainly from Bulgaria, Romania, and Ukraine and "who work for EUR 3 per hour, 60 hours a week, with no social security benefits" (European Parliament 2013a). Rather than addressing the abuse of the PWD in Germany and sending countries, the commission responded with the Enforcement Directive (ED) as a solution to the problem.

It is reasonable to say that the working conditions in the German meat industry—conditions predicated on a low-wage, posted worker employment policy taking place within a transnational legal gray zone—are an open secret. Some European businesses, such as Danish Crown, have relocated large parts of their business to make use of this "business model" provided by Eastern European workers (Wagner and Refslund 2016). As a result, within ten years, Germany has changed from a net importer of meat to a net exporter of meat. Germany is the largest producer of pork in Europe, with over 58 million pigs slaughtered annually (Chemnitz and Benning 2014).

The sector has undergone various structural changes, as well as a process of company concentration, since 1999. In the following, there have been remarkable shifts in the structure of the workforce. Between 1999 (when there were 186,717 jobs) and 2014 (when there were 143,138 jobs), almost 44,000 jobs subject to social insurance were lost in the field of slaughtering and meat processing (Federal Employment Agency [Bundesagntur für Arbeit, BA] 2015). This corresponds to a nationwide fall in employment by 23.3 percent (BA 2015). A native worker explained that those who lost jobs in the meat sector went on to work as truck drivers or in the cleaning services or in whatever came their way (interview with butcher, 2014). At the same time, the number of posted workers from Eastern Europe rose to "well over 25,000" (Brümmer 2014, 148). However, there are no precise figures on the number of posted workers in the sector. The two years with the largest reduction in jobs subject to social insurance were 2001 (when 11,837 jobs were abolished) and 2008 (when 12,339 jobs were cut nationwide). The number of employees subject to social insurance continued to decline in 2009 (−3,081) as well as in 2010 (−2,380) (BA 2016).

Slaughterhouses have traditionally utilized low-skill labor and a Taylorist form of work organization, which is still the case despite significant upgrades in technology. The meat slaughtering and meat processing companies have adopted strategies to reduce wage costs, which have led to deteriorating wages and working conditions in countries such as Germany and the UK (Grunert, James, and Moss 2010; Wagner 2015a; Wagner and Hassel 2016). German companies have mainly resorted to external flexibilization by employing posted workers. Posted and subcontracted workers mainly from Eastern Europe are employed in meat slaughtering and meat processing in Germany but are subject to social security contributions in the sending country. Registration requirements do not exist for posted workers. It is therefore difficult to calculate the exact numbers of posted workers. A works council survey conducted by the Food, Beverages and Catering Union (Nahrung-Genuss-Gaststätten [NGG]) in 2012 indicated that, in the large meat processing companies, posted workers accounted for up to 90 percent of the factory workers (NGG 2012). Another NGG works council survey indicated that, in certain other meat processing firms, posted workers made up 50–90 percent of the factory workers (NGG 2012). Of the 30,000 workers in the slaughtering industry, every third worker is employed under a subcontracting contract (NGG 2013). The use of subcontracting arrangements is itself highly contentious in the meat industry. Such arrangements require a service to be fulfilled. In the meat industry, this service is oftentimes formulated as "the smooth sequence at the conveyor belt" (interview with community initiative representative, 2012), offering an indication of the precarious use of these contracts to cut labor costs. Service contracts became attractive because a sectoral minimum wage had been long absent.

Because of the regulatory void (i.e., the nonexistence of the minimum wage), the NGG union was the first DGB affiliate to call for, as early as 1999, the introduction of a statutory minimum wage in Germany (from 2010 onward, the demand was for a minimum wage of €8.50/hour). The NGG union covers the entire hospitality, food, and beverages sector, with approximately 1.3 million employees (only insurable jobs). The number of union members is 204,348 (Güster 2015), which corresponds to a union density of roughly 15 percent. The employers' side is much more fragmented by subsector. The employers' association in the hospitality sector is the German Hotel and Restaurant Association (Deutscher Hotel und Gaststättenverband [DEHOGA]), and in catering is the Bundesverband der Systemgastronomie (BDS). In meat processing, by contrast, there is no single employers' association at the federal level but four different associations: the Food and Beverage Employers' Association (Arbeitgebervereinigung Nahrung und Genuss e.V. [ANG]); the Meat Industry Association (Verband der Fleischwirtschaft e.V. [VDF]); the Federal Association of the German Food Industry (Bundesvereinigung der Deutschen Ernährungsindustrie e.V. [BVE]); and the German Federation for Food Law and Food Science (Bund für Lebensmittelrecht und Lebensmittelkunde e.V. [BLL]).

Collective agreements in meat processing are typically negotiated at regional or (predominantly) at company levels—if they are negotiated at all. While the regional level is the most important level for collective agreements in most industries, the main difference between the meat sector and other sectors in the German economy is that, in the meat sector (though also in the food processing sector more broadly), every year hundreds of collective agreements are concluded and renegotiated at the firm and regional levels, leading to a very differentiated collective bargaining landscape. It was not until 2014 that the social partners in the meat industry were able to effectively negotiate a minimum-wage agreement. While the trade union NGG requested sectoral minimum wage negotiations, it did not have a negotiating partner because the big slaughterhouses were not members of the ANG. The primary reason why a minimum wage was agreed on was related to strong public pressure (for a detailed discussion, see Jaehrling et al. 2016). This increase in support for a minimum wage was taking place against the backdrop of the likely introduction, following the 2013 general election, of a statutory minimum wage in January 2015. To ease its introduction in low-wage sectors, particularly in East Germany, the federal government offered all affected sectors the possibility of agreeing to, for a transitional period of up to the end of 2017 at the latest, minimum hourly rates below the probable statutory minimum wage of €8.50. However, the precondition for such collectively agreed on variances was that the minimum rates thus agreed on would have to be declared generally binding. To that end, the meat processing industry was included in the Posted Workers Act (Arbeitnehmer-Entsendegesetz) (Doelfs 2014).

After lengthy and complicated negotiations (for a detailed overview, see Jaehrling et al. 2016), the sectoral binding minimum wage of €7.75 per hour was agreed on and came into force on August 1, 2014 (NGG 2014). Initially, the minimum wage in the meat processing industry was set to be significantly lower than the planned statutory minimum wage of €8.50 per hour with a steady increase. The collective agreement will remain in force until the end of 2017 and includes a declaration of commitment to further negotiations regarding a new minimum wage beginning July 2017. Trade unions, government representatives, and employers' organizations agreed that the establishment of the minimum wage is unlikely to reverse the trend to hire subcontractors, because the trend has become an institutionalized part of the meat industry (Hassel, Steen Knudsen, and Wagner 2016). While it will improve the legal terms and conditions for posted workers, the de facto rights of posted workers are oftentimes difficult to enforce because of the way firms are able to draw on different power resources and reinterpret rules in the absence of effective enforcement institutions, which will be discussed in depth in the following chapter.

Chapter 3

Management Strategies in Transnational Workspaces

Employing foreign subcontractors via the EU freedom of services is a relatively straightforward process. The main contractor signs a contract for the provision of a certain service with a foreign subcontractor for a pre-defined service and period. The contract lays down the time frame in which the product has to be produced or the service has to be finished, the price of the end product or service, and the liability agreements and tools employed to realize the service. In the construction sector, the contract would be concerned with a certain part of the construction process to be finished within a given period of time and for a certain end price. In the meat industry, the contract would refer to a certain cut within the slaughtering process in the slaughterhouses that is executed by a subcontractor for a definite amount. The price is determined by the subcontractors and offered in a competitive bid.

Within the production process, strict boundaries between the main contractor and the subcontractor have to be upheld. One works councilor from a slaughterhouse explained:

The main contractor has a skilled worker knowledgeable in meat cutting on its payroll. That person gives the order to the subcontractor. The worker tells the subcontractor, for example, today 6,000 pigs will be processed in the primary cutting and 6,000 pigs in the boning. The steps in this process— ham, shoulder, stomach, et cetera, et cetera—happen on different conveyor belts. The main contractor is not allowed to say how many of the subcontract workers are needed to do the job on the conveyor belts. It can neither say in which time frame the products have to be processed. The subcontractor manages the whole process. However, the skilled worker in meat cutting is standing next to it, and he can only talk to the person with the blue helmet, the foreman, from the subcontractor. Also, in terms of quality, he cannot say anything. He has to wait until the product is finished and can only then decline the end product. The main contractor knows that it will be very difficult to finish the order in time, with the same amount of people within the working hours available. But it is not allowed to say, "You need more personnel." This means the main contractor is aware that certain practices may take place to finish the order in time. (Interview with works councilor from a slaughterhouse, 2015)

In a similar vein, the boundaries in the construction industry between the main contractor and the service companies have to be respected. "The workforce of the different firms does not mix. We make contracts for certain services with subcontracting firms. For example, the services are for setting up the molds or for the pouring of the concrete for the walls and ceilings. In theory, we are not allowed to communicate with the firms doing this service. The contract states that only two foremen, one from each firm, can communicate with each other. The subcontractor is only there to get the order from us and communicate it to its workforce" (interview with works councilor from a construction company, 2012). In theory, this system creates clear boundaries between the main contractor and its subcontractors and, consequently, between the different workforces and the channels of worker representation. Even though posted workers work on the premises of a construction site or a slaughterhouse in Germany, the main contractor contractually excludes control over the quality of working conditions. The subcontractor decides how the service is rendered, how quality is ensured, and which normative framework for worker voice exists. This boundary-making between workforces of the main contractor and the subcontractor does not necessarily stop at the first level. More common than not is the development of subcontracting chains in which the first-level subcontractor outsources a service to another subcontractor, which may then outsource a service to another subcontractor, and so forth. One works councilor stated that "this is a big construction company and they have subcontractors. At some point, you lose the overview. The company is a bit smaller and is called x, y, and z but is doing the same thing. You know that, at least at the second subcontracting level, that something is not right, that people are not treated fairly" (interview with works councilor from a construction company, 2012). Long and ambiguous subcontracting chains evolve in which the boundaries between tasks and workforces begin to blur. In these spaces, regulatory voids occur.

This chapter will closely examine the regulatory voids present in these posting workspaces. Subcontractors and employment relations within these regulatory voids develop a normative framework of their own apart from the regulatory system that has been established at the EU and national levels. This regulatory void, this chapter argues, is upheld by the inability to change the norms within these workspaces via the current institutional setup in place. Actors such as trade unions, works councilors, and labor inspectors are aware of the different regulatory framework in a normative and empirical sense but are not adequately equipped to change the status quo. This observation is important because, even though a certain regulatory system has been created in Germany for posted workers, examining how a different parallel structure of norms is established and upheld is relevant for the political process. Therefore, while we know about the mechanisms of institutional change at the political level (Cremers, Dølvik, and Bosch 2007; Eichhorst 2000), we also have to pay close attention to the mechanisms that can initiate institutional change at the microlevel. Streeck (2009) notes that "one must pay at least [as much attention] to the micro level as to the macro level of social action" (254).

The aim of this chapter, therefore, is to study how microlevel societal actors such as firms, unions, works councils, and individual workers interact with the changing regulatory configuration. It studies how employers enact the posting framework creatively by circumventing rules. This chapter demonstrates how these mechanisms initiate a process of institutional change through power dynamics at the microlevel that are generally relevant for theories about institutional change. In pursuit of a more nuanced understanding of the regulatory dynamics of posted work, this chapter identifies the ways in which actors draw on different power resources to influence the outcomes of negotiations or to implement policies without negotiation at the workplace level.

The examination of how actors engage with an institution draws attention to the "gaps" between the design of an institution and its actual on-the-ground implementation and effects (Pierson 2004, 103). Taking my cue from Lipsky's 1980 classic study *Street-Level Bureaucracy* and Dubois's 2010 work on street-level bureaucrats, I look at how policy is renegotiated in the daily encounters of actors in the posting relationship. Lipsky (1980) and Dubois (2010) have both examined the vertical relationship between organizations strongly tied to national institutions and alerted to the high degrees of discretion and the relative autonomy that exists at the microlevel within nation-states. By contrast, the present study focuses on transnational institutional spaces.

My findings show that the possibility for firms to diverge from rules is accelerated in a transnational setting. Transnational worker posting offers employers an additional power resource due to the increasing inability of states to regulate (Lillie 2010) and enforce regulation in a cross-border work relationship (Wagner and Berntsen 2016), as well as because of the difficulties unions face in mobilizing posted workers (Hardy, Eldring, and Schulten 2012). Moreover, this chapter provides a microcosm for wider issues of institutional change. The outcome is similar to what Thelen (2004) has called "conversion" and Hacker (2005), in a very different context, has labeled "drift." In both instances, the institution remains formally intact while policies may change without formal revision, resulting in ground-level change (Hacker 2005). While firms officially adhere to the rules and thus leave them formally intact, they conceal their rule avoidance behind a facade of conformity. Firms divert the attention from the actual power dynamics and processes of change within transnational posting workspaces. This is relevant because the appearance of conformity is often sufficient to attain legitimacy (Oliver 1991). This in-depth study of context contributes to institutional theory by bridging the gap between institutional context and intentional action (Jackson 2010).

The posting of workers regulation creates not only a dual labor market in Germany but also a complex array of regulatory spaces where actors are able to enact policies according to their own needs and interests. The enactment of institutions depends not merely on the overall social context but also on the power dynamics between the actors shaping this context (Dubois

2010). Management creatively engages with the rule framework, whereas posted workers are structurally constrained from effectively resisting management practices in isolation from union representation. While a certain wage floor has been created for posted workers, we should be cautious in inferring from the seemingly compliant behavior of firms that they have internalized the normative order put forth by the rule makers (Dubois 2010). Rather, transnational workspaces adhere to regulatory dynamics of their own. The European provision of services has removed many possibilities for states to regulate their labor market or to properly enforce the regulations, thereby creating microworlds that produce autonomous rules. My argument is that, to adequately grasp the institutional mechanisms at work in transnational posting, it is necessary to look at changes in legal and policy settings complemented by examining power dynamics at the microlevel.

Microlevel Rule Enactment: Management Practices

The PWD and its national pendants purport how posted workers are to be regulated. In the posting process, a series of informal rules reflect "how things are done" alongside and even in contradiction to the formal framework. Several management practices exemplify how the posting of workers rules are circumvented at the microlevel; this is particularly true as discussed in the following:

1) Disregarding adherence to the maximum work period
2) Manipulating working hours to undermine the hourly minimum wage
3) Withholding annual leave pay
4) Circumventing minimum wage obligations by subtracting costs such as transport, tools (such as knives), and protective work clothing
5) Reducing social security contributions
6) Circumventing employers' obligations for work-related accidents
7) Financially exploiting workers through overpriced housing

Legislation in Germany requires written documentation of posted workers' contracts with detailed information on wages and working hours to be kept onsite in case of controls by the labor inspection Customs Enquiries

(Finanzkontrolle Schwarzarbeit [FKS]).[1] On large construction sites and in big slaughterhouses, firms' accounting books will mostly adhere to the maximum working hours and pay. On the surface, then, it would seem as if transnational subcontractors adhere to the existing institutional framework; however, when special attention is paid to the enactment of institutions, a different picture emerges. Several unionists expressed that, nowadays, "on paper, all the employment standards are correct," but there is "a difference between the rights on the one hand and the reality on the other. Workers operate in what can be described as a lawless space" (interview with IG BAU representative, 2012). One unionist described the current practice on German construction sites as not what one would "consider classically as 'illegal,' that is, undocumented workers. Companies deceive the respective institutions on a whole new level by manipulating the working hours of workers, deducting accommodation pay from the worker's wages, and thereby circumventing the minimum wage standards" (interview with IG BAU representative, 2012).

Actors adhere to the rules artificially on paper. Instead of officially breaking the rule, they enact the rules differently from the intentions of the rule makers. One of the many cost-saving strategies of service providers is the deliberate manipulation of working hours. For example, posted workers work 240 hours a month, while the employer accounts for only 160 hours in the paychecks, thereby reducing the actual hourly wage (interview with IG BAU representative, 2012; interview with NGG representative, 2012). Posted workers from various countries working for diverse service providers on different construction sites and in slaughterhouses confirm this practice. One worker explicitly stated that "all the workers get five or six euros per hour, and the main contractor knows and supports this" (interview with Polish posted worker, 2012). This practice disregards the adherence to the maximum work period while simultaneously undermining the hourly minimum wage. Even though workers earn an hourly wage on their paychecks, they do not receive overtime, nighttime, or weekend bonuses on top of their wages. Working one hundred hours of overtime without being paid accordingly reduces their hourly minimum wage to €5–6.

Manipulating the time allotted for breaks is another way to influence overall working hours. One works council representative in the meat industry pointed out the "ability [of management] to manipulate working hours everywhere. Even if workers have to check in with a chip card, one can always say, we have [let them have] long breaks in between" (interview with works councilor, 2015). Similarly, on construction sites, the chip cards are not tamperproof. Data collection of the working hours of workers at the construction site is conducted via the main entrance. In some cases, workers work for twelve hours on the construction site, yet only eight hours of pay show up on their paycheck; the justification that follows is that workers were given four hours' worth of breaks during the twelve-hour work day (interview with IG BAU representative, 2015).

These practices are very difficult to detect because the paychecks and accounting books list the legally allowed maximum number of hours worked. In addition, management requires workers to attest in writing that they receive the minimum wage payment (interview with management representative, 2012; interview with posted worker, 2012). Controls by the FKS do occur; however, official controls are not able to detect malpractices because the paperwork of foreign firms is in accordance with the rule system. "Controls take place every two years at the big slaughterhouse firms" (interview with works councilor, 2015). The works councilor of a large slaughtering firm pointed out that "more is not manageable by the labor inspection. Most of the time, the labor inspection looks at the books, does a couple of interviews with workers who say that all is well because they don't want to lose their job, and then they leave again" (interview with works councilor, 2015). This observation was repeated time and again in various interviews with trade unionists and works councilors and exemplifies the different normative system posted workers and institutional actors in Germany are embedded in.

Moreover, all workers on German construction sites are entitled to annual leave pay. The collective social fund Sozialkassen der Bauwirtschaft (SOKA-BAU) was established to ensure that workers receive their holiday entitlements by raising contributions from the employers and granting benefits to employers and workers. However, employers deduct the holiday payment from the collective social fund from the workers' wages. A Spanish posted worker described that "the SOKA-BAU system is well conceived from the German legislator, and no one can circumvent it. And now there is the big but: SOKA-BAU transfers the accumulated holiday payment for the workers to their service provider. However, my employer does not pass the vacation pay received from the SOKA-BAU on to the workers. And that is unfortunately the practice" (interview with Spanish posted worker, 2012). The vacation pay system as envisioned by the rule makers imposes useful rules on the payment of vacation pay to posted workers. However, the way it is appropriated turns its purpose completely upside down. Instead of guaranteeing the due vacation pay for the workers, firms make a profit.

Circumventing minimum wage obligations by subtracting costs from the pretax payments subcontractors receive from the contracting firm is another profit-making strategy of service firms. In the meat industry, deductions for using the knives to cut meat or withholding small sums of pay for wearing appropriate clothes for the cooling chambers are some examples of ways to lower the promised wage level. One worker noted that the daily rate for using the clothes for the cooling chambers provided by the main contractor was between 0.16 and 0.30 cents a day (interview with butcher, 2014). In a similar vein, construction firms may charge workers for using the tools they need to fulfill a service. In both industries, charging workers for transport costs—required to take the workers to the worksite and back to the housing site—is another way to reduce the end amount of the promised salary. For workers, these practices create a legal uncertainty and a blurring of distinction between formal and informal rules because firms create a normative environment in which these practices appear to be legal. Thus, it is possible for employers to avoid following the host-country rules; these loopholes even present a way to conceal the emergence of deregulated spaces in which no regulation at all is upheld.

This is equally visible in the case of tracing the social security contributions of workers across EU member states. Before posting a worker from one member state to another, the posting company has to fill out and submit an A1 form (proving that the worker is registered in the sending country's social security system and that the employer has paid social security contributions in line with the worker's wages—including wages earned in the sending country). This reduces social security contributions by insuring workers in the sending country, where these premiums are lower. While posted workers report the deduction of social security pay from their salary in the host country, this amount does not appear in the sending country social security contributions of, for example, Poland or Romania. For example, a paycheck of a Romanian posted worker displays a number of irregularities: besides not specifying the working hours or hourly wage, the social security contribution (e.g., unemployment, health, and pension) and over-hour premiums are not specified; however, they are deducted from the net salary under an umbrella term, "payments in country of origin," though without actually paying into the social security institutions in the country of origin.

Grave consequences occur in cases of workplace-related accidents. In one case, in which the employer told the workers involved that he was paying the due employer contributions to their health coverage, the firm did in fact not do so in practice (interview with posted worker, 2012). While some posted workers reported that colleagues who had accidents were sent home, others disclosed that they were let go in case they did need to get an operation from a work-related accident. While sometimes the pay for the day of the accident was reimbursed, the workers did not receive reimbursement for the resulting period in which they were too sick to come in to work (interview with Polish posted worker, 2012). The subcontractor employing workers on German territory is responsible to adhere to the health and safety standards of the workplace and cover the workers' health insurance. These examples hint at the fact that these forms of labor mobility since the enlargement of the EU have been accompanied by the emergence of new forms of inequality stretching beyond the work sphere into the social and even private sphere but also into the living spaces of workers.

Accommodations are generally linked to posted workers' employment on a certain site and with a specific employer and can be arranged in a way that allows for high levels of temporal flexibility and extended working hours. Posted workers are usually accommodated in what has been called a "dormitory labor regime" (Pun and Smith, 2007) where "workers live next door to a factory so that they might always be on call for work" (Rainnie, McGrath-Champ, and Herod 2010, 300). The term was established in the context of today's Chinese production regime. The function of these dormitory labor regimes is to "capture single migrant workers for short periods of tenure in order to maximize the utilization of labor services during the working day" (Smith 2003, 334). This aspect of extended control is similar in the case of posted work when, for example, meat factory workers reported that they were picked up without notice for an additional shift (interview with posted worker, 2012). The living spaces vary greatly in form and quality. Workers are often housed in apartments, in houses, or in bungalow/camping parks together with colleagues. The accommodation may be in urban, industrial, or rural areas. In some cases, workers reported that the housing site does not fulfill standard health and safety requirements. Employers charge extensive amounts for rooms and, in some cases, even for daily use of a mattress. Subcontracting firms themselves have set up parallel housing businesses in Germany to exploit the housing needs of their workers. On the paychecks, deductions from the net salary also include rent for housing.

These practices show the discrepancy between the rule system as envisioned by political actors and its appropriation by posting firms. While it is possible to describe this system as outright illegal, which it is, and to call for better enforcement, this chapter shows that stronger enforcement would not necessarily change the status quo; the parallel rule system created under the strategies of the service firms is being created and preserved through the interplay of unequal power relations between workers and transnational firms, through posted workers' isolation from trade union structures, and through the inability of the labor inspection to detect rule-breaking and enforce compliance.

Worker Perceptions

Norms are related to the types of workers firms employ. A firm's policies on, for example, hours of work will be important in developing a set of norms around what firms expect from workers (Smyth et al. 2011). Rules or norms between posted workers and employers can establish that certain practices, even if technically illegal, are perceived as bending—though not breaking—the rules. This agreement oftentimes deviates from the regulatory norms of the host country. There is a discrepancy between the norms of the host country and those of the home country in terms of what is expected from the employer's side as well as what is acceptable from the employee's side. In certain cases, for posted workers maintaining the norm structure, the wages and employment conditions they agreed to before taking up the employment are more important than upholding the rule system of the host country. One posted worker explained, "Our firm told us what to say when controls take place. We agreed to that before we came to Germany. That's normal. If someone offers you to work in Germany for €8.50 and you earn €3 in Poland, then you agree, even if €8.50 is less than the German minimum wage. Management also told us that we would not receive vacation pay, even though the contract states that we do" (interview with Polish posted worker, 2012).

In the meat industry, a worker posted from Romania explained a similar situation: "When we signed the contract, we knew that the amount on paper would not match the wages we would actually get. We agreed to a lower wage even before we came here" (interview with Romanian posted worker, 2012). The worker continued: "We did not even receive the amount that was promised to us, and the working hours and housing conditions are terrible" (interview with Romanian posted worker, 2012). Migrants may be relatively tolerant toward substandard employment conditions due to a so-called dual frame of reference (Waldinger and Lichter 2003) within which they compare employment terms abroad with job opportunities at home. Given the difficulties of collective agency, workers tend to be reluctant to challenge poorly regulated employment relations and, instead, opt to accept a certain level of precariousness in their employment conditions. This mental framework occurs within the context of a heterogeneous European labor market and welfare state situation. Significant wage differentials and social security contributions exist between the member states (Höpner and Schäfer 2008). The reasons posted workers take up work and accept certain employment conditions vary, ranging from experiencing unemployment in the home country, to needing to pay debts or pay for medical procedures for family members, to simply looking forward to being able to afford a better life (interview with posted worker, 2012). Workers are afraid of losing their employment if they voice grievances.

Working in a highly competitive job market may also force workers to accept substandard conditions, as the alternative is no job at all. Even workers with decades of experience abroad indicated that they sometimes sign employment contracts without having them translated into a language they can understand: "If I don't accept it, someone else will come. Everyone is easily and readily replaceable" (interview with Polish posted worker, 2012). In the face of limited job opportunities at home and higher earnings abroad, working in transnational workspaces is for most migrants a strategy to materially improve their situation. Even though these workers may be conscious and critical of exploitative firm practices, this does not readily translate into resisting these practices outright.

More often than not, posted workers feel that exiting the employment relationship is the only viable option to alter their situation. Structural limitations, economic deprivation, and isolation from union structures constrain worker resistance, leading to "a sense of powerlessness at the collective level" (Mrozowicki and van Hootegem 2008, 201). According to one Romanian worker, it was difficult to establish solidarity because of the many nationalities at the plant; moreover, the workers were engaged in industrial-ized work for the first time and were intimidated by management: "There was no trade union for us, no one told us our rights, and, once we asked for them the employer said, if you don't like something, we will send you right back home" (interview with Romanian posted worker, 2012). The same is true for work-related accidents. One worker recalled that a colleague was not able to show up for work one day and, immediately, the foreman of the firm showed up and ordered her to pack her bags, leave the premises, and go back to Poland (interview with Polish posted worker, 2012). The worker stated: "He just fired her because she was not able to work for one day and therefore did not show up for work" (interview with Polish posted worker, 2012).

People formulate various forms of association at work, such as friend-ships, ties of solidarity, and informal pressure groups through which they develop norms that govern their behavior within the workplace setting (Mills 2002). In that sense, the behavior of the workers is connected to the type of workplace and the workplace culture they are embedded in. Moreover, it is also connected and upheld by what Mills (2002) calls "sense-making events." In the present case, these sense-making events refer to management intimi-dation and economic constraints or unemployment in the home country. These sense-making events are paired with individual notions of conformity to the environment workers are placed in, resulting in the enactment of a particular framework that, in this case, diverges from the regulatory post-ing framework at the EU and national levels.

Segregated from native workers in the workplace, posted workers are often subject to less favorable employment conditions than their native counter-parts. Still, the employment conditions of native workers are also influenced by the changing world of the European labor market. When asked if loyalty still exists between workers, a native worker in the meat industry replied:

No. The only thing that matters is the price. The salary difference between native and posted workers was . . . we [native workers] got €0.80 for a pig shoulder depending on the cut. Today, posted workers do the same for €0.35, which is way below half the price per piece rate. Sure, if I don't have to pay social security benefits in Germany, I can calculate a totally different price. This is how the whole structure developed. According to EU law, firms could do what they want in terms of the price. EU rights do not count for anything. Workers accept any practice. I don't understand how all the practices can take place in Germany. Other EU countries are also influenced by the practices that re-occur in Germany—their sectors go broke because they cannot compete. It is unfair to the other countries. The people are unemployed without any perspective. (Interview with native butcher, 2013)

The share of migrant workers holding union membership remains low due to short job tenures at particular workplaces, unfamiliarity with local institutional structures and collective actors, language barriers, and the fear of being dismissed for union activities (Berntsen 2016). Interaction between posted workers and unions does occur but is mainly limited to certain dire cases. Even though workers on occasion express anger about their situation, they fear employer retaliation and feel powerless to claim their rights. These are decisive factors that deter workers from interacting with the union or reporting management malpractices to the authorities.

Reinforcing the Status Quo

While the trade unions have sought to establish closer relationships with transnational posted workers, they face considerable obstacles to interacting with workers at the workplace level, including language barriers, the frequent site mobility of workers, and workers' fear of and lack of trust in unions. These factors reinforce the persistence of the employment practices as unions oftentimes try to enforce the regulations in place without the support of the transnational posted workforce. If workers try to cooperate with the union, they are often exchanged quickly with other workers and sent to another worksite (interview with IG BAU representative, 2011). This intimidates the new workforce even more, and the union in such an instance will find it very difficult to get in touch with the new workers (interview with IG BAU representative, 2011). One unionist explained: "If you ask workers what they earn, they always say, out of fear, the respective minimum wage. And then you stand there and think: 'Well, if the people are paid minimum wage, we cannot do anything.' Everyone knows that this is not the case. I cannot report this to the media or the labor inspection because workers are afraid to talk" (interview with IG BAU representative, 2011).

The union in the meat sector similarly tries to interact with posted workers by distributing flyers in the native language on workers' rights. At first, the union thought that language barriers were the foremost problem, which could be overcome by distributing flyers and employing union secretaries that speak mainly Eastern European languages. These efforts so far had not resulted in increasing worker commitment toward the union. One unionist explained: "I can understand that they don't think it is important to join our union because they are here short-term, but, for us, this means that we will not continue to put resources into organizing posted workers, if the strategies used so far were not effective" (interview with NGG representative, 2015).

This union perception reinforces the isolation of posted workers from union structures. Likewise, worker fear hinders meaningful interaction with the union and sustains certain management practices. This leaves considerable leeway for subcontracting firms to disrespect certain posted workers' rights (interview with IG BAU representative, 2011). The complex relationship between management practices, worker fear, and union isolation constrains the ability of the labor inspection to detect malpractices. The task of the labor inspection is to check the hours worked and wages paid to posted workers in the firms' accounting books, which must be kept on the construction sites at all times. According to an official from the labor inspection, there is rarely a discrepancy. However, this official suspects that the actual accounting book is kept in the host state (interview with labor inspector, 2012). One labor inspector explained: "Companies in principle commit to paying the minimum wage, but we know that there are, I would almost say, hundreds of ways to circumvent it. For us, it is of course difficult. It is almost impossible for us to investigate in their home country, that is, to investigate in Poland. I'm not saying that it is entirely impossible, but it is almost impossible. Generally, there is a blatant mismatch between the costs and expected benefits, in most cases" (interview with labor inspector, 2012).

Moreover, a works council representative in the meat industry noticed that time and again subcontractors would forget the accounting book in another office or in the host or home country and, thus, ask the labor inspection to send their book within the next day. However, the works councilor noted, "It hardly takes 24 hours to change the books. The books are mostly handwritten with pencil. Workers may have to countersign, but they will always do so because of the fear of losing the job" (interview with works councilor, 2015).

The union, the labor inspection, and works council are aware of the practices that *appear* to be legal but actually circumvent the rights of posted workers. According to a government report, many subcontractors in the construction as well as the care and cleaning sectors avoid paying salaries according to the minimum wage regulations (Deutscher Bundestag 2013). The report identified that controls do occur but only to a minimal extent because they are extremely time-intensive and complicated. Two reports by the DGB identified mechanisms to avoid minimum wages in construction that are similar to the findings of this book. For example, the manipulation of working hours oftentimes results in the payment of wages close to what workers would earn in their home country instead of the host country's minimum wage (Siebenhüter 2013; Dälken 2012).

Moreover, the enforcement of rights is difficult due to the limited control mandate and staff shortage of the FKS as well as the lack of transparency created through long subcontracting chains (Dälken 2012). These practices are widespread in construction, but similar avoidance mechanisms occur in other sectors, for instance, in the cleaning and care sectors (Dälken 2012). The central association of the German building industry ZDB confirmed the existence of gaps in the regulation (Zentralverband deutsches Baugewerbe 2006). Mechanisms such as double-bookkeeping across borders make it very difficult for the FKS to detect firms' avoidance mechanisms (Zentralverband deutsches Baugewerbe 2006). Interviews with the union representatives as well as with employers confirm that, while a relatively dense institutional framework exists, the capabilities of the labor inspection to detect malpractices in these transnational workspaces are severely limited.

Institutional Change through Rule Enactment at the Microlevel

The interaction between host-state and home-state institutional frameworks and norms creates a space in which actors can draw on different power resources to enact policies without official negotiation at the political level. This is especially relevant for institutional change because the meaning of an institution is constantly reinvented, in this case, by posting actors (Streeck 2011). To understand the creation and evolution of an institution, it is important to examine the context as well as the intentional actions of actors, as they are mutually constitutive (Jackson 2010). Institutions are defined here as formal rules that actors can use dynamically to realize their aims (Streeck and Thelen 2005).

The literature on institutional change identifies different modes of change under the categories of "displacement," "layering," "drift," and "conversion" (Streeck and Thelen 2005). In the variant of "displacement," newly introduced behavioral patterns gradually or completely replace the original institution. "Layering" refers to practices that do not replace old ones but are added to already-existing institutions. Changes occur because the new additions cumulatively transform the initial operation of the institution in a relevant way. "Drift" describes institutional settings in which the institution as such remains intact but changes in the environment are not adequately addressed. The absence of adjustments leads to significant changes in the operation of an institution. Similar to drift, "conversion" refers to an institution that remains formally intact but is used, by way of interpretation or different application of its properties, for a purpose for which it was not originally intended. The forms of change most relevant for the empirical material discussed in this chapter are similar to conversion and drift. In both instances, the institution remains formally intact, and policies may change without formal revision, causing ground-level change (Hacker 2005; Thelen 2004). To understand the incremental process of change dynamics at play in the posting relationship, it is useful to combine these mechanisms (Barnes 2008).

Conversion, like drift, can be considered a process of adaptation in which the institution itself does not change but is exploited to serve new ends (Thelen 2000). Even actors not involved in the institutional design may circumvent or subvert rules when they are in opposition to their own interests (Streeck and Thelen 2005). In this mode of transformation, actors have a greater space in the institutional reproduction to reassess their interests and contemplate institutional change (Streeck and Thelen 2005). The real meaning and function of an institution ultimately emerges only in the course of how it has been interpreted and practically applied by actors. Rules and their enactment converse "through deviant local enactment or the slow accumulation of anticipated or unanticipated consequences of an institution's routine operation" (Streeck 2009, 125). This is possible because institutional rules are left ambiguous as a result of political compromises, and the balance of power between actors shifts (Jackson 2005).

In the case of transnational posting, firms use the lack of strong union presence or the ability of labor inspectorates to enforce regulations to redeploy familiar institutions in ways that undermine their logic of action. Practices such as double-bookkeeping across borders hinder the proper monitoring of the labor rights of posted workers. This creates an ambiguous space in which it is difficult to disentangle which rights are adhered to because circumstances change and practices are fluid. The firm strategies discussed here are similar to what Oliver (1991) labeled "avoidance" in her research on strategic responses of organizations to institutions. Avoidance in this context can be defined as "the organizational attempt to preclude the necessity of conformity; organizations achieve this by concealing their nonconformity from institutional rules or expectations" (Oliver 1991, 154). Nonconformity is hidden behind a facade of compliance: firms officially adhere to the rules and thus leave them formally intact. However, they reappropriate them in a different manner by manipulating working hours and consequently undermining the minimum wage.

This is important from an institutional perspective because, as Oliver (1991) remarks, the appearance of conformity is often sufficient to attain legitimacy. These practices result in a situation of conversion: while the regulation was originally implemented to hinder the underbidding of wages in the construction sector, it now becomes an instrument to place workers in direct wage competition next to each other in an ostensibly legitimate manner. The inability of unions and the labor inspection to control these practices shields firms from the enforcement mechanisms in place. While the rules are officially adhered to and not formally altered, the original intention of the institution is reversed by not paying the due amount or by not passing on the vacation pay that is due to the workers.

Drift is closely related to conversion but differs from it because, under conversion, the implementation and use of institutions change, whereas, under drift, the changing environment alters the effect of institutions (Hacker 2005). Institutional drift occurs because of long-term shifts in the institution's environment. The effects of institutions change because they do not adapt to the newly emerged structure (Hacker 2005; Streeck and Thelen 2005). In relation to transnational posted work, the facts of the matter show the insufficient adaptation of union and rule-enforcement mechanisms. Borders exist between IG BAU and posted workers because of language barriers, high labor turnover, and worker fear. In similar contexts, unions have been criticized for their ineptitude at finding ways to organize and represent vulnerable workers (Jenkins 2013). The union's inability to adapt to the changing environment, on a national or transnational level, isolates posted workers from interest representation and hinders the detection of the avoidance of collectively agreed-on institutional practices. Union dissatisfaction with limited worker interaction runs the risk of reinforcing the borders between workers and the union, contributing further to a drift between the design of the institution and its coverage. Drift also occurs because of the inability of the labor inspection to effectively control employment standards or enforce fines across borders. The union and labor inspection interviews both show that the regulation cannot be fully enforced within the current framework. While a pan-European labor market was created, the institutions that enforce rules have not been adapted effectively, creating multiple institutional segments that float like driftwood next to each other without being able to interact.

Ultimately, the process of institutional change is initiated by these practices. New interpretations of existing rules emerge and gradually displace the old. Caused in this way, however, deviations from traditional interpretation and application of practices are often merely matters of degree. If over the course of time these small changes are used by more and more actors and reinforced by further deviations, this can add up to larger discontinuities. The result is a "sort of incremental institutional change that proceeds independently from the intentions of those supposedly in control" (Streeck 2009, 125). The empirical material described here offers a snapshot of an ongoing larger process. Combining different modes of change can help disentangle the current process of transformation.

Nevertheless, the ultimate consequence of eroding institutions through, for example, drift might result in a situation in which an institution gradually breaks down over time and "withers away" (Streeck and Thelen 2005, 29–30). In April 2014, the European Parliament adopted the ED of the PWD. Its main purpose, as the name indicates, is to ensure that there is consistent application and more effective enforcement of posted workers' rights contained in the 1996 PWD. It is important to note that the final version of the ED of the PWD was not negotiated via the co-decision procedure. Rather, the final text was decided via the trilogue. The trilogue negotiations are a formal procedure in EU law and most often take place when the Council of Ministers cannot agree to the proposed changes from the European Parliament through the co-decision process. One advantage of the trilogue is that it speeds up the decision-making process. In this case, the European Commission and the European Parliament wanted to arrive at a quick decision because the ED needed to be agreed on before the elections of the

European Parliament in 2014. The disadvantage of the trilogue is that it basically leaves the negotiations to a few actors that agree on a final text. Further negotiations with other actors, at this point, no longer take place. Moreover, in these negotiations, the European Commission's endorsement is particularly important in light of the fact that, if it opposes an amendment the European Parliament wants to adopt, the council will have to act unanimously to accept that amendment. In the trilogue on the ED, representatives of the European Parliament, the council, and the commission attended these informal tripartite meetings. The agreement reached in the trilogue was informal and "ad referendum." Therefore, the European Parliament approved the final text in its formal procedure in April 2014 (for the implications of the ED, see chapter 6).

The literature on institutional change has highlighted the dualization of the posting of workers labor market induced by policy adjustments (Menz 2005). This chapter has shown how transnational firms are able to circumvent this re-regulation in isolation from union and labor inspection control. Processes of institutional drift and conversion help to interrogate local practices and dynamics of change, which form an important foundation to examine further processes of change at the aggregate level (Fiss and Zajak 2004). Unequal power dynamics are played out at the workplace level, resulting in complex relations between employers, workers, unions, and enforcement institutions. The findings presented here suggest that national institutions have persisted, but actors reappropriate them differently than initially intended, launching a process of change. The institutional framework is formally adhered to, concealing nonconforming practices.

Incremental changes in the European labor market have opened up loopholes that management can exploit. Transnational firms have identified creative ways to avoid regulation, and posted workers are oftentimes not able to oppose these malpractices due to fear of employer retaliation, structural limitations, and/or isolation from union structures. This leads to a process of conversion in which institutions remain formally in place but are adapted by firms to serve their interests. This process of change strongly depends on the interests and power of actors that make decisions in organizations. Transnational workplaces can be considered political arenas in which different actors engage with and contest rules, drawing on unequal power resources (Fiss and Zajak 2004). Even though the union and labor inspection are aware of these malpractices, they lack the resources to detect and prosecute rule circumvention. Employer strategies to exploit gaps in regulation tend to weaken these traditional sources of power. The concept of drift can illustrate the multiple spheres of regulation that exist between unions and workers and their inability to sufficiently interact to close the gaps in the regulation in order to counter management practices.

While the regulatory framework claims to establish a rights framework for workers, it allows its circumvention through its many loopholes. The practices in transnational posting are the result of the tension between the claimed needs of a flexible labor market and the desire to closely monitor employment of mobile workers. Castles (2004) argues that migration "policies that claim to exclude undocumented workers may often really be about allowing them in through side doors and back doors, so that they can be more readily exploited" (223). Transnational posting provides a low-cost pool of labor that facilitates the "flexibility" of the labor market while appearing to adhere to the institutional setting. The negotiated policy framework is being neglected by transnational firms due to the inability of states to enforce policies across borders and the inability of workers and unions to interact in a labor market characterized by high mobility, labor turnover, and exploitation.

From the perspective of employer strategies and labor market outcomes, transnational labor posting is often complementary to other institutional change dynamics in the German labor market. While the traditional German model still covers a significant proportion of workers, a complex labor market of low-wage workers outside that system has grown (Bosch and Weinkopf 2008; Palier and Thelen 2010; Thelen 2009). Firms now regularly use outsourcing to smaller firms as a way to avoid works council and trade union power (Doellgast 2009). Microlevel studies in other sectors in the German labor market also allude to avoidance mechanisms similar to those in posting. For instance, so-called mini-jobbers (temporary workers employed on a €400-a-month basis) often do not benefit from the tax and social security exemptions they are legally entitled to in the retail sector, while employers make a profit (Voss-Dahm 2008). Other studies have revealed that mini-jobbers are regularly being denied lawfully guaranteed sickness and holiday pay (Benkhoff and Hermet 2008). In a similar vein, Jaehrling and Méhaut (2012) explored the gaps in regulation for atypical workers in the retailing, hotel, and service sectors that led to precarious employment practices and rule avoidance. This suggests that the findings presented here may be representative of broader trends in the German labor market, whereby loopholes in the regulation and the growth of weakly organized sectors allow for discrepancies between context and enactment.

While posted work and its national and microlevel regulation are embedded in deep structural changes in the German political economy, it does add another dimension to the debate. New exit opportunities created through the EU freedom of services undermine current regulatory practices and union power. This provides firms with leeway to creatively exploit regulatory gaps in their cross-border activity. The process of change is still in flux and up for contestation. Conclusions about the ultimate extent of the modes of change have to remain preliminary. Nevertheless, the findings here point to a process in which surface compliance is substituted for deep compliance. The picture that emerges is one of a variegated labor market in which concealed nonconformity drifts alongside institutional host-country systems of worker representation and rule enforcement.

The union's aim to extend the regulation to posted workers has been achieved at the policy level but has been adapted differently at the microlevel. On a day-to-day level, posted workers and the union do interact, but meaningful engagement is not taking place in the traditional sense of migrant workers becoming union members. Unions have had past successes representing, organizing, and including immigrants in their ranks (Milkman 2006; Fitzgerald and Hardy 2010; Eldring, Fitzgerald, Arnholtz, and Hansen 2012; Connolly, Marino, and Martinez Lucio 2017), but the increasing share of flexible workers from abroad, who have neither the intention nor the possibility (yet) of settling in the country or job where they work, remains a group that trade unions regularly fail to reach. Against this background, the next chapter discusses the impact of this institutional space on posted worker voice.

Chapter 4

Posted Worker Voice and Transnational Action

Territorial boundedness and coherence have long served as the backdrop for the efficient functioning of industrial relations institutions. Europeanization, however, has arguably started to disassociate, or de-territorialize, the bonds that tied trade union structures to fixed spatial configurations. In Germany, unions are struggling to adapt to these new challenges while also aiming to "re-territorialize" their relations with labor migrants. Re-territorialization implies the reinsertion of an element previously extracted from one context (what is called de-territorialization) into another. While a certain destruction takes place during de-territorialization, it also opens up the opportunity for re-territorialization. De-territorialization in its most useful sense therefore forces us to think anew about how territorial configurations are challenged and rechallenged (Ó Tuathail 1998; Cox 1997; Brenner 1999). While European integration, globalization, and the economic crisis have put trade unions under pressure, these economic and political integration processes have also provided unions and workers with new possibilities to organize resistance (Bieler et al. 2015).

Through an exemplary case, this chapter traces the process and explores the conditions under which re-territorialization can evolve in these transnational workspaces. The present case examines an alliance in the meat industry between transnational posted workers, a local civil society organization, and the trade union NGG. From an analytical perspective, the chapter considers these coalitions as examples of re-territorialization that is a form of resistance in increasingly de-territorialized labor markets (Pile and Keith 1997). The case study concerns a group of Polish posted workers employed in the German meat industry who are resisting precarious management practices. A local community initiative, the NGG, and the media played a major role in facilitating resistance. The case demonstrates that the transnational nature of posted workers' employment relationship and living situation requires a different approach to organizing resistance beyond the traditional institutional perspectives on German trade unionism. The case goes against arguments that German trade unions conventionally refrain from forming coalitions because of their institutional position and Germany's strong employment law. This chapter addresses the following questions: Under which conditions are posted workers able to exercise voice when traditional channels of representation are absent? How can we explain a shift by a trade union in a national context in which it is usually uncommon to mobilize labor migrants at the grassroots level in coalition with civil society actors? Under which circumstances are these coalitions successful?

The case contributes in a number of ways to findings from other studies of union strategies toward posted workers and labor migrants (among them Berntsen 2016; Berntsen 2015; Danaj and Sippola 2015; Krings 2013; Bengtsson 2013; Tapia and Turner 2013; Lillie and Greer 2007). In doing so, it aims to enhance understanding of the challenges and limitations for traditional and nontraditional actors in a pan-European labor market. It highlights the shift in German unions' strategy from social partnership to coalition building (Greer 2008). Parts of the German industrial relations system correspond less and less to the image of an institutionally embedded German trade union secured by a stable framework of employment law. This points to within-country differentiation of power resources as regards the bargaining power that trade unions can mobilize in relation to the employers and the state (Korpi 1998). Therefore, the case demonstrates the conditions under which such coalitions emerge and are successful, and how posted workers can be embedded in the host-country institutional system and voice concerns in situations where traditional channels of representation are inefficient. Moreover, it emphasizes the importance of engaging with migration and its different configurations in relation to industrial relations (Berntsen 2015; Çaro et al. 2015; Marino 2015; Lee, Tapia, and Turner 2014; Wagner and Lillie 2014; Alberti, Holgate, and Tapia 2013; Alho 2013; Krings 2009; McGovern 2007; Fine 2006; Holgate 2005; Milkman 2006; Wills 2004).

The chapter proceeds as follows. First, the EU-induced de-territorializing tendencies in the posting labor market as well as the re-territorialization possibilities for trade unions are explored. The following section presents a case study on transnational action in transnational workspaces. These insights contribute to our understanding of how unions can interact with labor migrants in an era when labor mobility is both intensified and politically contested (McGovern 2007), and how far these relations contribute to renewed union solidarity (Le Queux and Sainsaulieu 2010).

De- and Re-territorialization in the Context of EU Worker Posting

De-territorialization

Posted workers, even though they are working in the host-country territory, are disconnected to a large extent from that country's institutional system and labor relations. Posting disentangles the borders, tying economics, politics, and culture to fixed spatial configurations. In the posting of workers discussion, "de-territorialization" denotes the decontextualization of labor law and industrial relations systems from particular territorial ties (Mundlak 2009). The EU de-territorializes capital and labor from the restrictions of national regulatory systems (Bailey 2010). This context poses a challenge for industrial relations, working and employment conditions, and modern unions because these institutions evolved in symbiosis with the nation-state and are also extensively regulated by national legislation (Streeck and Hassel 2003). Collective bargaining, just like labor market regulation, was territorialized by embedding a legal pattern within and through the state, with its coverage usually limited to employers and workers within the territory's borders (Mundlak 2009).

European integration gave employers the option to exit territorial regulation, as discussed in the previous chapter, but this has equally impacted the voice functions that have been established within bounded nation-states as well as the ability of trade unions and works councils to organize and represent workers. Employing posted workers via subcontracting arrangements does not trigger a claim to equal treatment internal to the main contracting firm. A main contracting firm develops internal norms of reciprocity and fairness between workers and management, culminating in, for example, works councils and a regulatory framework of workers' rights and voice within that firm. These norms follow an internal organizational logic only partly dependent on outside context (Doeringer and Piore 1971; Grimshaw and Rubery 2005). Subcontracting arrangements enable companies to exit from the norms established within these contexts. For example, subcontract workers are not allowed to interact with the works council of a main contracting firm, usually a German firm in which firm-centered works councils exercise workers' voice at the workplace level. Subcontracting arrangements therefore exist in interaction with recruitment in certain national markets and are used to keep different groups of workers organizationally and legally apart (Wagner and Lillie 2014).

Posted work does not simply alter the German institutional framework and social regulation but rejects them wholesale by embedding posted workers in an institutional system other than the German one (Wagner and Lillie 2014). Firms exiting traditional voice mechanisms thus should impact trade unions' and works councils' ability to organize and interact with workers. However, some argue that the institutional embeddedness of German unions and a "framework of employment law [that] has remained broadly supportive" (Frege, Edmund, and Turner 2004, 146) restrain unions from alternative ways of organization and representation, such as by seeking coalitions with community organizations, mobilizing workers outside the usual tool of the strike, and framing issues in terms of social justice (Baccaro, Hamann, and Turner 2003). While Krings (2009) argues that trade unions in Germany are unlikely to change their modus operandi in response to EU labor migrants because they have a strong institutional position and will therefore refrain from building coalitions with civil society organizations, the findings here point to a change in strategy as a necessity.

For the trade union and for the works councils, organizing posted work points to several difficulties. One difference in organizing native workers as opposed to transnational posted workers is the familiarity (or lack thereof) present between the firms and the workers, which may complicate access to the worksite for organizing purposes. With the liberalization of the provision of services, one unionist mentioned that new and unfamiliar firms have entered the labor market. "It is practically like this: if the employees are at a German construction company—depending on the size—there is either a works council, who we [the union] talk to a lot, or we know the smaller firms, not necessarily because of in-depth contact, but at least [we know] the name and its reputation and [we] can make an informed assessment. But if I somehow hear of a firm that I have never heard of, then we do not know what is going on there, and we do not know the conditions, and it is difficult for us to help and make an assessment of the situation" (interview with IG BAU representative, 2012). With the increase in subcontracting, trade unions have lost their organizing base in some firms completely. If no organized members are present in the core firm, in a slaughterhouse, or at a construction site, then the union is not allowed to enter the premises. When the union has members in the permanent staff, then it is allowed to enter only for certain purposes, which constrains the actions trade unions can take (interview with NGG representative, 2012; interview with IG BAU representative, 2012).

If a works council is present, the trade union will try to access the site via the main contractor's works council because the subcontractor employees have neither works councils nor relations to trade union structures. In the German metal industry, works councils of core firms have sometimes used their power to influence industrial relations conditions in contractor firms. For example, IG Metall was able to negotiate an in-house collective agreement for posted workers at the Meyer Werft, as will be explained further in chapter 6. However, an employee representative in construction explained that it is "illegal" to represent employees further down the subcontracting chain in construction because they do not belong to "their company" (interview with works council representative, 2011). Workers from the main contractor and from the subcontractors may not "mix," as this would be suggestive of using temporary agency work, which is (mostly) prohibited in construction. The only possibility for the main contractor's works council to communicate with the posted workers is via the posted workers' supervisor. The standard way to inform a posted worker about a health and safety breach on the site is to "notice the defect, communicate it to the supervisor, who informs the workers about it" (interview with works council representative, 2011). This invokes neither direct contact with the workers nor interest representation. While German subcontractors also operate under the same limitations, their workers have the right to establish their own works council—at least in principle.

An added difficulty, as pointed out in the previous chapter, is the lack of widespread organization of posted workers due to various factors, including language barriers, fear of employer intimidation, and therefore partial compliance of the firm with the de facto rule system. Workers oftentimes accept substandard employment because of experiences of unemployment in the home country or because of cross-country wage differentials. The workforce is often unfamiliar with or rarely seeks the help of collective channels of representation (interview with NGG representative, 2013). Posted workers, even though they are physically in the host country, often frame their understanding of their employment rights in the context of their home country. One posted worker explained her embeddedness in the home country and her excluded status in the host country: "I have been to a union meeting once. There are certain rights, but [they are exercised] in vain because they are not applicable to us [posted workers] because we are not employed by a German company but by a Romanian company. Our rights are connected to the country and firm where we are employed and pay taxes and social security contributions to, that is, Romania" (interview with Romanian posted worker, 2012). The worker's impression was that there is a dividing line based on the national context of where the employer is based, inhibiting the enactment of certain rights and preventing her from seeking representation from the trade union in the host country. Moreover, many posted workers mistrust unions because of negative experiences with home-country unions or misunderstanding the union structure in Germany. The worker leaves the sending country geographically but, in a regulatory and normative sense, carries its institutional rules and normative system into German territory. The predicament is that, while unions are understaffed and lack the resources to mobilize posted workers, the workers themselves also mostly refrain from seeking help from the union because of fear of employer intimidation and retaliation. This results in a dilemma: both the union and the workers are inhibited from changing the status quo (Wagner 2015a). Although workers are aware of their agency in this context, they also know that changing their situation is difficult and risky because of the multiple mutually reinforcing barriers as well as the relative helplessness of the unions to protect them. As labor's channels of influence decreased and low-wage worker posting has intensified, trade unionists have responded by building coalitions with societal actors. The case illustrates a complementary approach to examine how resistance unfolds in transnational workspaces under conditions where traditional avenues to protest are blocked or marginalized.

Re-territorialization

Transnational workspaces need not be spaces of exclusion. Resistance may re-territorialize spaces in various ways to transform their meanings and "enable [them] to become a space of citizenship, democracy and freedom" even within limits (Pile and Keith 1997, 30). The margins especially have been discussed as sites of resistance. Other forms of regulation may also produce "other" voices (Hetherington 2003). The re-territorialization process arises from the re-embedding of elements into a different context. In this case, re-territorialization could mean disembedding posted workers from the meat industry's (absent) regulatory framework, which lacks collective action (de-territorialization), and re-embedding them into an inclusionary framework with collective interest representation. In the traditional industrial relations literature, collective bargaining is viewed as a process aimed at re-embedding an otherwise oppressive environment (Colling and Terry 2010; Katz, Kochan, and Colvin 2008). Where no such channels exist, employers resist power sharing, and workers may require a more active mobilization to promote their interests and win acceptance of collective representation (Tapia and Turner 2013).

To a certain extent, the challenges of including posted migrants in collective channels of representation revealed the weakness of the trade union itself (interview with NGG representative, 2013). To counteract these processes, the union started to form coalitions with local groups (interview with NGG representative, 2013). An example of such a coalition, as well as the conditions under which it was able to develop and be successful, is explored in the following section.

Power Relations in a German Slaughterhouse

This case involves a group of 82 Polish posted workers. These workers were employed by a Polish second-level firm doing a contracted service for a

German first-level firm at a slaughterhouse in Germany. The factory had 1,100 employees in 2012, of which 50 percent were core personnel and the other half were externally employed. Of the external employees, 90 percent were subcontracted and 10 percent were agency workers (interview with management representative, 2012). The largest nationality groups of the posted workers were Polish, Romanian, and Hungarian (interview with works council, 2012). Owing to long subcontracting chains, neither the management nor the employment counselors of the main contractor were aware of the second-level subcontractor or the working conditions of its workers.

The workers' contracts stated that they would receive an hourly wage of €7.50, with additional overtime, night, and weekend work bonuses. On arrival, they were paid €4 per hour with no bonus pay. Moreover, they were treated like a highly flexible source of labor. The supervisors decided late every evening which workers were assigned to work the following day. At times, the workers were transported to the factory only to learn that no work was available that day, and, consequently, they did not earn any wages. Some of the workers worked in the meat slaughtering halls and others in the meat packaging section. The employer organized the transportation to and from work; on various days, workers had to wait hours for transportation back to their housing site after a 10- to 12-hour shift. The company did not pay social insurance and sick pay as promised to the workers (interview with community initiative representative, 2012). In a severe case, a woman who suffered a work accident was sent back to Poland, and the lack of treatment resulted in permanent disability (interview with community initiative representative, 2012).

Moreover, the living conditions for the workers were substandard. On arrival, the workers were confronted with empty flats, and they had to collect furniture from the bulk waste on the street. Eight to twelve workers had to share a two-room flat. There was no gender separation in the flats, and a person close to management lived in each flat so as to watch the workers in their leisure time. In the factory, the workers were not provided proper work clothes: even though the clothes adhered to the hygiene standards of the factory, they did not protect the workers against the cold in the cooling chambers where the meat was cut and processed. Solidarity was difficult to establish within the work team because of high labor turnover and management oversight in their living spaces (interview with Polish posted workers, 2012).

Furthermore, the workers were engaged in industrialized work for the first time and had no prior experience in collectivism. Such attitudes worked in concert with workers' unfamiliarity with the union structure in Germany, fear of employer retaliation, and lack of appropriate contacts (interview with Polish posted workers, 2012). Employees had few options for expressing discontent other than unilateral exit. The material motivation for taking up the work in Germany—mostly related to paying off debts, experiences of unemployment in the home country, or being able to finance medical procedures for family members—increased the workers' dependency on the job, and the low-skilled nature of their work placed them in a poor bargaining position (interview with Polish posted worker, 2012).

A "Moment" of Transnational Action

The labor practices in the meat factory received local and later national attention when the posted workers shared their grievances with a local community initiative. The initiative was created in 2006 and consisted of ten volunteer activists, who also financed the incurred costs. Most of the volunteers were employed in the care sector. From its outset, the initiative raised a scandal over the arbitrariness of companies and entrepreneurs against their employees in the state of North Rhine-Westphalia. Using media pressure, it organized public solidarity around, and supported local work disputes on, for example, the unlawful termination of works councils or the improper use of "one-Euro jobbers."[1] While the community initiative had experience in mobilizing workers and creating public solidarity, by 2012 it had not yet interacted with hypermobile EU workers.

The posted workers' housing sites were based in the same town where two activists from the community initiative lived. The story began when the two activists became aware of the posted workers' situation by chance. One activist, a native Polish speaker, overheard a conversation among the Polish posted workers in a local store and started to make conversation. In the opinion of the activist, trust was established because of their shared nationality and language, and, having herself immigrated to Germany many years before, she came to be regarded by the workers as a confidant (interview with community initiative representative, 2012). Meeting a fellow native Polish speaker served as a catalyst for the workers, who shared their grief about their work and living conditions.

The initiative informed the union from the beginning about the workers' situation. Ideological positions influenced the likelihood of the emergence of the coalition. The activists were trade union members themselves. They believed it to be important to include the NGG in the process. Together, they decided that the community initiative would try to establish further contact with the workers and keep the union informed. The initiative sought contact with workers over a period of several months by repeatedly visiting their housing site and distributing flyers with information about the workers' rights. Finally, contact with a group of six workers was established by entering the housing site without management noticing. The workers trusted the two activists and repeatedly visited the activists' home on Sunday afternoons. Together, they looked at their contractual situation and tried to decipher which rights the workers had and how they could claim them (interview with community initiative representative, 2012).

In response to the workers' precarious working situation as well as their dependency on employment, the initiative decided to enact a strategy of media attention. The aim was to present the case in a social justice framework to win public support. The initiative used informational materials from the trade union and later depended on the union to negotiate with the employer. They also started to organize a strike in front of the meat factory; however, management response resulting from the media pressure made the planned strike unnecessary. By exposing the employer's treatment of workers and publicizing the substandard living conditions of the workers' housing, the media strategy created public solidarity. Because a municipal building company owned the workers' apartments, the activists were able to put pressure on local politicians and win their support in the debate. Moreover, the initiative created an online database with detailed information on the main contractor, the subcontracting firm, and the municipal housing company, as well as employee testimonies about their deficient working conditions. The aim was not just to document the situation but also to create easily accessible information that media and political actors could draw on. Addressing local politics was thus an essential strategy in the procedure. With the workers' consent, the activists released a press statement about the workers' precarious working and living conditions. The local and national media responded immediately.

While the workers' initial step to alter their working conditions was to secretively meet with the community initiative, their transformative act was to speak out in a television documentary put on by a national public broadcaster. While one worker agreed to give an anonymized interview in front of the camera, others distracted management and guarded the door in order to allow the journalist to film their apartment. Both the documentary and the media coverage by local and national media included "shaming" the main contractor as well as bad publicity for the municipality that hired out the flats to the Polish subcontractors. Meanwhile, the community initiative and the NGG prepared for a long battle that would bring company abuses to the public eye, embolden employees, and force major concessions on their behalf.

However, after the airing of the documentary on nationwide television, the main contractor terminated contractual relations with the Polish subcontractor. At this point, the NGG became more formally involved in the process, organizing a meeting with the main contractor and the posted workers to clarify their grievances and negotiate the further employment of the workers (interview with NGG representative, 2012). The outcome was the takeover of the whole workforce by the German agency firm that had previously contracted the Polish subcontractor. The workers were now employed under a German agency contract. Here the agency collective agreement (between the Association of the German Temporary Work Association [Interessengemeinschaft Deutscher Zeitarbeitsunternehmen, IGZ] and the DGB) applied. The main contractor was forced to make an arrangement with the German agency firm to take on the workers because the localized work stoppage would have caused wider disruptions to the production process. In that sense, the workers, in tandem with the community initiative and the media, were able to exert "workplace bargaining power" (Silver 2003, 13).

From the workers' point of view, the material gains—in this case, higher wages and improved employment and living conditions—were significant. Moreover, workers did not need to feel threatened or intimidated by management anymore and had a fixed monthly income and proper work clothes. Despite the fact that they were still used as a highly flexible source of labor, the workers appreciated that their work schedules were not as unpredictable as before and that their employment contract was prolonged. Their employment context changed from being excluded from the host-country institutional framework to being included through their employment at a

German agency firm. Taking further legal action against the employer would have jeopardized the workers' future employment and, thus, outweighed their gains.

Varieties of Re-territorialization

German industrial relations institutions are marked by a tension: the power of these institutions ends at the territorial border, while the free mobility of services and labor enables regulations to extend across these borders (Wagner and Lillie 2014). These shifting boundaries of regulation are a mechanism for firms to segment the labor market. While immigration generally tends to undermine industrial relations institutions by reducing trade union control over the labor market, in the past, trade unions have coped by integrating and organizing immigrant workers into their structures. This process has not been without its problems and tensions, but there has nonetheless been a trend toward integration of immigrants into the trade union movement (Marino, Roosblad, and Penninx 2017). In the expanding postwar economy, unions created a position of strength for themselves. While largely unskilled migrant workers were recruited to do the most arduous and worst-paid jobs (Pries 2003), they were working in sectors where unions were organizationally and institutionally anchored. However, today, the German economy and the German trade union landscape are not the same as they were a couple of decades ago. Trade union efforts to integrate and represent migrant workers are now embedded in industries that have experienced radical growth in precarious employment, rapid weakening of the unions in the industry, and widespread workforce segmentation of both native and migrant workers (Wagner 2017). Actors play a major role in defining these spaces through their ongoing interactions. It is a mutually constitutive relationship between the material facts of the EU legal framework, the ideas held by actors about the organization of these spaces, and actors' practices manifesting those ideas.

Searching for ways out of this situation, the DGB and its sectoral unions have undertaken various initiatives aimed at integrating migrants into worker representation structures. For example, IG BAU has responded to increasing numbers of posted workers by attempting to organize and represent them. One well-known effort was the establishment of the European

Migrant Workers Union (EMWU), which attempted to create a transnational structure, separate from the national trade union structure, from which workers could receive representation in both home and host countries. The idea was to create a structure in which workers, who may be represented by trade unions in their home country, could move to another country and be represented by the trade union in that country without switching membership or paying double fees; the goal, then, was to overcome the boundaries that exist between worker representation in the EU. The IG BAU proceeded to create this structure by establishing a separate institution as a sort of daughter of the IG BAU (interview with IG BAU representative, 2011). The idea was that trade unions in different EU countries would support this organization with a fee contribution that would help create a network in which workers could be represented when crossing borders. For example, a Polish worker who moves from Germany to the Netherlands would be represented under the framework of the EMWU regardless of the national union structure. However, the EMWU did not establish the independent role for itself it initially envisioned. On the one hand, it faced insufficient union support, with some unions not wanting to create separate institutions next to the already-established national institutions (interview with IG BAU representative, 2011). On the other hand, it faced significant organizational flaws and was eventually reintegrated into the IG BAU (Greer, Ciupijus, and Lillie 2013).

The IG BAU continues to represent the rights of posted workers at the political level, provide information to workers on construction sites or at housing sites, and help with legal services in certain dire cases. In fact, the IG BAU equally recognizes the importance of forming coalitions with other actors to highlight and improve the situation of posted workers. One IG BAU representative stated, "In the case of health and safety violations, institutions pay far too little attention. Especially when posted workers or seasonal workers from abroad are involved. Only trade unions, some journalists, church representatives, and some civil servants are interested in their situation; the rest ignores it. The main issue is cheap labor, it does not matter how [it is acquired]. The colleagues are often afraid to be a witness, and the relatives in the sending country are often not told what happened in the country of work" (interview with IG BAU representative, 2012).

Moreover, the DGB has responded to increasing numbers of posted workers by establishing "fair mobility" service centers in large cities across

Germany. In these service centers, project workers with relevant language skills inform migrant workers (including posted workers) about labor laws and social legislation in their native languages and across sectors in an attempt to preserve the norms of the German labor market. The creation of the fair mobility service centers complements the recognition that migrant workers also need help with housing and other social issues. The service centers interact with other civil society organizations to help workers not only with employment but also with social issues confronting them. The centers do not focus on a particular sector and are not part of a trade union; rather, they simply employ staff with relevant language skills. However, they are supported by and closely cooperate with trade unions and other NGOs to cater to the needs of labor migrants or facilitate contact with other organizations. The fair mobility centers are financed by the DGB, national funds, and European funds and operate on a project basis.

In a similar vein, Lower Saxony created service centers within civil society organizations wherein project workers with relevant language skills inform posted workers about labor laws and social legislation in their native languages and across sectors. Lower Saxony supported this cooperation because, in the area of its jurisdiction, an especially large amount of meat production occurs, which, as we have examined, is often paired with exploitative practices toward posted workers. The project workers cooperate with the NGG on a daily basis. This development is in fact part of a larger trend in Germany to establish coalitions between trade unions and civil society organizations to build solidarity with the posting workforce.

Discussion

Mobile labor is attractive to transnational capital for several reasons. A very particular "spatial fix" (Harvey 1982) is based on the use of migrant mobile labor usually without local family ties. Mobile workers are, per their definition, not rooted in the local community and have not been socialized into the traditions of the regional working class. They therefore lack the source of power local communities and workers' organizations may provide (Rainnie, McGrath-Champ, and Herod 2010). While today's geographic places should be conceptualized as intersections of partly global circuits (Massey 1994), it is still the case that localities or geographical proximity may support the transfer and thus convergence of workers' demands and the emergence of mutual support or collective action. Recruiting mobile labor can be regarded as a way to cut off such power resources. The effect of using mobile labor is strengthened by strategies to keep individuals or groups of workers divided. Language barriers and cultural differences do in fact separate mobile workers, as do, in more extreme cases, the forms of accommodation and surveillance they are placed in and under. However, workers draw strengths not only from industrial relations institutions but also from social interactions with community leaders, religious associations, and other local social ties (Lier 2007).

A case in point is the case study presented in this chapter, which illustrates that in response to the isolated and precarious position of posted workers, a local community initiative and the local NGG office developed a strategy around changing the employment situation of the workers. In contrast to established German labor practices based on relations of social partnerships punctuated by occasional episodes of collective bargaining conflict, this campaign privileged extensive media publicity, social coalition building, and local political pressure. In this sense, certain features of the campaign resembled the logic of so-called social movement unionism. This type of unionism refers to a strategic orientation propounding that unions should form coalitions with other progressive social forces (Johnston 2002). The union began to look for alternative sources of power by building coalitions with societal actors and by finding issues that appealed to the broader public. Extensive publicity included the "shaming" of the German main contractor by drawing attention to the new forms of "slavery" within a highly industrialized country such as Germany, pleading for a larger understanding of social inequality. Furthermore, publicizing the municipal building company's role in providing housing to the workers' employer contributed to putting pressure on local politics. These efforts were led by a small group of volunteer and union activists.

As Staggenborg (1986) points out, "Understanding . . . the conditions under which coalitions emerge and succeed in advancing movement goals is crucial" (374). The conditions influencing the coalition were, among others, related to a shared ideology (McCammon and Campbell 2002). The community initiative was sympathetic toward trade unions and thought it crucial to establish the connection. Moreover, the trade union appreciated the work done by the initiative because the union itself faced several constraints. Almeida and Brewster Stearns (1998) have noted that, in cases of resource shortage, groups may seek out coalition partners, because an alliance with another group can sometimes provide them with the means to accomplish their goals. For the trade union, it can be problematic to interact with posted workers because of the absence of a common language or general lack of staff, and hiring additional personnel is oftentimes not possible due to budgetary constraints (interview with NGG representative, 2013). Cooperating with other organizations helps solve this dilemma. For the initiative, drawing on union informational materials and knowledge during the negotiations with the employer was helpful due to its lack of resources in this regard.

Moreover, the weak political position of the NGG was a catalyst for it to seek partners for help in pushing its agenda. Otherwise, the lack of impetus may have left its strategy unchanged. In certain cases, a lack of political opportunities as opposed to their presence, as argued by some authors (Diani 1990; Staggenborg 1986), may actually spur coalition building (McCammon and Campbell 2002). Overall, the success of the efforts by all sides was strongly influenced by a social justice framework that won media attention and broad public support, including among local politicians. This development can, however, prove problematic if we conceive of the mass media as agenda-building instead of as a mere instrument or resource for activists—an entity that can privilege certain groups over others and structure the chances for discursive success (Blanco 1997). Similar coalitions are increasingly forming in other regions where meat factories are present as well as nationwide in the context of organizing posted and labor migrants more broadly.

The mobilization of posted workers depended on the flexibility of the community initiative, the language skills to foster mutual communication, and, to a certain extent, the trust related to a shared identity. According to the community initiative, it was able to act and react more flexibly than the local union office (interview with community initiative representative, 2012). The proximity to the workers' housing site facilitated frequent visits. Moreover, due to the migratory background and shared language between the workers and one of the activists, the workers' trust was more easily established than would have been possible for the local union officers. Another important catalyst was that the community initiative served as a shield for the workers' anonymity. While the trade union can generally protect anonymity, it has to reveal the workers' identities in, for example, more formal legal proceedings owing to the absence of collective redress in Germany. Nevertheless, it was important that the NGG stepped in to formally negotiate the takeover of the workers with the employer because the trade union was able to draw on experiences with employers' negotiations and established contacts with the main contractor. New, experimental strategies may aim not only to revitalize previously existing institutions but also to build them (Turner 2009). As a result of the nationwide effort to increase media pressure on politics to act by exposing the precarious employment and living conditions of workers, local governments funded service points for posted workers and the formation of an employers' association that negotiated a sectoral minimum wage, which helped place the issue of statutory minimum wages firmly on the political agenda (Behrens and Pekarek 2012). In that sense, union ability and willingness to form coalitions with societal actors depended on the country, the nature of the employment structure (national or transnational), and industry-specific factors. In the case presented in this chapter, posted work in the German meat industry not only illustrates the alteration of the German institutional system but also rejects the German institutional framework and social regulation wholesale by embedding posted workers in an institutional system other than the German one (Wagner and Lillie 2014). In the meat industry, as employers have broken with patterns of cooperation and transnational workspaces have increased, the NGG has sought alternative forms of leverage. The case therefore illustrates an alternative approach to transnational action in the German setting based on forming coalitions with other social actors in an experimental way.

In this context of transnational posted work, the short-lived nature of the transnational action was effective because it was able to address the immediate needs of the posted workers. Owing to their temporary employment status in the host country, they were not looking for an institutional channel representing their long-term interests; they simply needed a voice mechanism that would help them alter certain modes of management conduct (interview with Polish posted worker, 2012). Transnational collective action took place through local ad hoc organizations when certain problems needed to be addressed. Even though workers did not act out established scripts of collective worker resistance, such as joining the union or initiating a legal case against the subcontractors, their act of resistance was constituted by challenging existent forms of management conduct (Isin 2009). Contrary to conventional claims, labor migration is not necessarily a purely voluntary process (Cohen 1987). The interviewed posted workers came to Germany not because of some enthusiastic embrace of freedom of movement but because of socioeconomic problems, most notably low wages and unemployment in the home country, but also so that they could pay off debts, pay for medical procedures for family members, or simply afford a better life. For the workers, the balance has to be struck between retaining employment and covertly countering certain management conducts.

This case of transnational action did not cause an overall liberation from the unequal power relations within the pan-European labor market. Even though the workers' position in the labor market improved, they still navigate a highly flexible labor market, moving from one short-term contract and low-paid job to the next. Their lived experience can still be classified as a low-paid, easily replaceable source of labor. Their employment contract was extended for one month, but their employment status afterward remained uncertain. Contact between the union, the community initiative, and the workers disintegrated. However, Berntsen (2016), drawing on Katz 2004, points to the importance of recognizing migrants' nuanced processes of resistance such as "reworking," which is when migrants perform many acts that can be considered "accumulative . . . practices which materially improve someone's position, though do so within the confines of existing social and power relations and without attempting to change underlying power imbalances" (5). Moreover, in this process, some of these workers may have gained valuable experience in collective organization and may be more predisposed to collective orientation in their next employment post (MacKenzie 2010). Even short-lived transnational labor alliances could still be useful for the purposes of transnational action (Brookes 2013). After all, transnational solidarity does not develop automatically but is the result of concrete struggles (Bieler et al. 2015). While economic competition is certainly an obstacle to union action, it may also initiate it, since unions were in any case founded as a counterforce to the commodification of labor (Erne 2008).

The findings of this chapter contribute to a growing literature revealing blind spots in comparative cross-national perspectives based on institutional equilibrium. Findings in different institutional contexts such as the UK, France, Germany, and the Netherlands identify fundamental similarities underlying the mobilization efforts of previously unorganized groups of workers (Bertossi 2010; Gumbrell-McCormick 2011). In Germany, trade unions have adopted organizing tactics similar to those found in the UK to incorporate contingent workers into collective channels of representation (Vandaele and Leschke 2010). Moreover, a similar observation has been made in the French context with regard to immigrant workers more generally (Tapia and Turner 2013). Other studies on trade union and posted worker solidarity in the Netherlands have shown that modes of mobilization, such as media exposure and access to new resources and instruments of power, required coalition building (Berntsen and Lillie 2016). In France, increased alliance building between trade unions and other civil society actors has been observed to counter exploitative practices affecting posted workers (Lefebvre 2006).

The cases point to common dynamics in today's form of capitalism and the opportunity structures to counteract the current tendencies. This chapter suggests that this case study as well as other case studies in similar contexts can be viewed as advances to re-territorialize deregulated labor markets. Re-territorialization as resistance may take place as a reaction against injustice, but it may also involve a sense of "dreaming of something better" (Pile and Keith 1997, 30). By trying to resist, it is also possible to imagine or dream that resistance is possible, advancing the search for alternative worlds. The commonality between the different findings makes clear how unions mobilize "invisible workers" in the face of increasing employer opposition (Baccaro et al. 2010). These case studies can enhance our understanding of the opportunities and challenges for unions and workers in an era of increased labor mobility.

The possibility for posted worker resistance is embedded in the deep structural changes in the European labor market. Novel transnational workspaces are being created in the EU, and we need to investigate not only how labor power resists these at the policy level but also how workers are able to claim their labor rights in the absence of collective labor power in these marginal spaces. Traditional avenues of resistance have become difficult to access for transnational posted workers in the German meat industry. This chapter has challenged the understanding of German unions being constrained by the institutional framework to seek coalitions with societal actors (Kitschelt and Streeck 2003).

This case study has provided a case in which posted workers were able to exercise voice through channels largely uncommon to the German institutional framework. In the German meat industry, the weak institutional position of the trade union as well as the porous posting regulation led the trade union to seek out new, experimental strategies. While trade unions have largely been unable to mobilize this workforce, in this case, a community initiative stepped in to fill the gap. This case demonstrates that the transnational nature of the posted workers' employment relationship and living situation requires a different approach to organizing resistance beyond the traditional institutional perspectives on German industrial relations.

Several conditions underlay the emergence of the coalition. First, the need to share resources (flyers) and the possibility of dividing the work according to ability/expertise (the mobilization by the community initiative and the formal negotiation with the employer by the NGG) were preconditions for the cooperation. Second, achieving the NGG's goals required seeking out new partners. For posted workers, it was possible to exercise voice in the absence of traditional channels of representation because of the time-intensive and flexible approach launched by the community initiative, as well as shared language skills and, to a certain extent, a shared identity. Also, it was important that the parties involved had a particular workplace bargaining power, as the employer may have reacted differently otherwise.

Similar coalitions are increasingly forming in other regions where meat factories are present as well as nationwide in the context of organizing posted workers and in relation to labor migrants and contingent workers more broadly. This suggests that the findings presented here may be representative of broader trends in the EU labor market, whereby loopholes in the regulation and the growth of weakly organized sectors call for a more nuanced understanding of labor differentiation. This case is able to provide a microcosm of the conditions under which resistance may unfold in poorly regulated workspaces where traditional avenues to protest are blocked or marginalized.

More reflection is needed; different forms of power and labor markets, such as posting in a pan-European labor market, may call for different forms of resistance. This has some critical implications at the level of employment relations and labor market reform. To improve the conditions of permanent, temporary, settled, and mobile workers alike, changes are needed in the current forms of labor opposition, especially in non- or less-unionized and highly flexible sectors within which traditional forms of protest are undermined or marginalized. Acknowledging different forms of labor differentiation is a key step in this process for industrial relations actors and allows them to support alternative modalities of resistance in poorly regulated workspaces. Future research may further investigate whether these practices will undermine or coexist next to more traditional forms of resistance, as well as whether new alliances can be formed in this process.

Chapter 5

Borders in a European Labor Market

For many EU citizens, the reality of a borderless Europe is within reach, but for a large group of people, this reality seems farther away than ever. The European Single Market certainly created an institutional space with strong debordering tendencies for people, goods, services, and finance. Even if certain borders have disappeared, there has also been a multiplication of "new" and/or a shift of "old" borders. And even though we know that borders are everywhere and come in different guises—ranging from formalized state borders to borders within a city or the workplace—the actual function of borders is notably ambiguous if we look at different kinds of laws in the EU. The opaque nature of borders, it seems, is due to the persistence of the actual geographic lines that demarcate EU nation-state territories; this ambiguity interacts with a deregulation of borders for, among other things, goods, information, and professions that are contributing to the formation of new types of borders.

The pan-European labor market is a more concrete example of how these bordering processes intersect. In both theory and practice, the border for the movement of persons and services within the EU is no longer consistent with the edges of the physical territory of the member states (Christiansen and Jørgensen 2000; Zielonka 2000; Geddes 2005; Guild 2001). Borders still exist, but they are increasingly recognized as "fuzzy" (Christiansen and Jørgensen 2000), permeable (Zielonka 2000), and possibly not that important (Christiansen and Jørgensen 2000). While the discussion on EU integration and rebordering has highlighted how EU integration impacts the territorial structuring of politics, it has done so mainly from the vantage points of the state or the supranational levels (Zielonka 2000; Del Sarto 2013; Kostadinova 2013). However, the borders of and within the EU are not just produced by the Council of Europe or the European Commission; they are reproduced, constructed, and given meaning by different institutions and people. For example, the rebordering process of states intersects with the trend to outsource production in certain industrial sectors. The reconfiguration of the traditional form of the organization of the state and of the employment relationship embedded in and organized around bounded nation-states (Emmenegger et al. 2012) requires the examination of the complex relationships actors find themselves in across national contexts (Jackson, Kuruvilla, and Frege 2013).

This chapter explores the position and creation of borders in a pan-European labor market from the bottom up. It studies the reshaping of the nation-state from the microlevel points of view of societal actors such as mobile workers, public administration officials, firms, and trade unions (Radaelli and Pasquier 2006). Findings demonstrate that two types of borders are significant in relation to posting in a pan-European labor market: (1) borders for labor market regulation that inhibit the enforcement of labor rights and (2) the border of the firm—that is, the border between the main and subcontracting firms that isolates workers from the host-country industrial relations systems. These borders impact the institutional separation between posted workers and host-country trade unions. The European Single Market created permeable borders for firms and workers, but these borders were created by chance. The chapter discusses how firms strategically use and exploit the significance of national borders in the posting relationship and how this affects the workers' employment situation. While capital can take advantage of permeable borders, national administrations and organized labor cannot, impeding the effective enforcement of workers' employment and social rights.

Three key areas of study—the changing nature of state borders, institutional analysis, and the industrial relations literature on transnational solidarity and labor geography—provide important theoretical insights into the overall complexities of employment relations in the EU today. Separately, these literatures have yet to provide a coherent theoretical framework through which to comprehend the current labor market structure in a pan-European labor market. Combining their insights is a useful way of thinking about the shape of the current EU labor market, as labor migration is a decisive field in which the New Europe will be forged (Pries 2003).

The chapter is structured as follows. It starts with a discussion of the spatial reconfiguration of the EU labor market with regards to the regulatory framework of posted work in the EU and Germany as well as the theoretical understanding of borders in relation to this book. Next, it examines how borders to regulatory enforcement are created and how they intersect with the reconfiguration of firm borders, as well as the implications of these re-bordering processes on transnational solidarity. Finally, the chapter links the empirical findings of this book to the discussion on the territorial structuring of labor markets in the EU.

The Spatial Reconstruction of EU Labor Market Regulation

Transnational posted work opens up the opportunity to literally post a particular part of labor regulation from one "bounded" nation-state to another, allowing companies to "import" labor that is regulated, at least in part, according to the labor regulation of another "bounded" nation-state. The authority of an EU member state lies to a certain degree outside existing state borders. For example, a Poland-based company can legally offer to send its employees to Germany to process a certain amount of meat for a certain amount of time at a German slaughterhouse. Its employees perform their work as subcontractors as part of the production process in the larger meat factory in Germany, but their employment rights—and potentially their wage level if no generally binding minimum wage exists—refer back partly to the sending country's standards. In that sense, labor markets are not confined to a national space as to how they are regulated and how labor rights are enforced. The ability of states to seal their borders, the sine qua non of sovereign states, is therefore restricted; as a result, borders become porous.

However, bordering is not always the business of the state. Different actors such as citizens, NGOs, or employers are active in constructing, shifting, or erasing borders (Rumford 2008). These borders are not created at the edges of the nation-state but are configured throughout society. The European order is multilayered, instead of state-centric, and requires a new way of thinking about borders (Zielonka 2000) and their construction through various actors. This reconfiguration of borders is more about different regimes of rights than about managing population flows (Zielonka 2000). In relation to posting, an important actor in creating borders, strategizing around state borders, and creating different regimes of rights is the firm. The changing nature of national borders intersects with the trend to outsource production in certain industrial sectors. Not only has rebordering occurred—and is still occurring—at the nation-state level through EU-induced re-regulation; it also takes place at the firm level due to the firm's perceived need to adapt to market pressures. Posting occurs in sectors characterized by a fragmented production process through a specific division of labor between large contractor firms and small and medium-sized subcontractors. In Germany, this is particularly the case in the meat and construction sectors. This enables employers in Germany to hire foreign workers under different employment conditions depending on the seat of the service provider to cut labor costs, even though these employees work in the same workspace as native workers performing similar jobs (Lillie 2010).

The story of posted work is embedded within a manifold of developments that are simultaneously at play within the European and global economies. The fragmentation of, for example, manufacturing and service delivery processes has resulted in a disintegration of employment on a global level that has taken a variety of forms (Gereffi, Humphrey, and Sturgeon 2005). For instance, foreign direct investment or cross-border offshoring usually implies that labor processes are stretched across country borders, leading to a divided and geographically separated workforce frequently in competition with each other for jobs. Moreover, the increasing externalization and relocation of service functions have initiated a trend toward the outsourcing and relocation of front-office activities in customer service, back-office tasks, high-end software development, and other divisible domains in business processes (Huws, Flecker, and Dahlmann 2004; Batt, Holman, and Holtgrewe 2009; Taylor 2010; Flecker and Meil 2010; Coe, Dicken, and Hess 2008).

As a result, labor in the workplace is increasingly fragmented, and is further exasperated by the presence of workers employed by subcontracting or outsourcing service provider companies and temporary work agencies (Marchington et al. 2005). The main focus of analyses within approaches that are being called "Global Value Chains" or "Global Production Networks" is on the relocating or offshoring of work of transnational companies with the aim of tapping national, regional, or local labor markets with lower wages, higher flexibility, or laxer health and safety regulations (Coe, Dicken, and Hess 2008). In the Single European Market, labor and capital mobility coincide with the fragmented employment relations processes. To put it differently, both capital and labor are mobile in the transnational workspaces where posted workers are present. Capital mobility in this context is not motivated by access to local labor markets, because it involves mobile labor in the first place.

Outsourcing and atypical employment forms have eroded the inclusiveness of the standard employment relationship, a core element of the post–World War II institutional context in European economies (Bosch and Weinkopf 2008; Gautié and Schmitt 2010). Cross-border employment relationships add an extra dimension to labor market segmentation because posting does not take place within a "bounded" nation-state context but crosscuts both territories and the employment institutions and labor market regulations that have been established around these nation-state territories. The move away from the traditional form of the employment relationship embedded and organized around bounded nation-states (Emmenegger et al. 2012) requires the examination of organizational and social relations that underpin the complex relationships actors find themselves in across national contexts (Jackson, Kuruvilla, and Frege 2013). Previously fixed borders have shifted, creating complex interactions between different types of actors across a variety of national contexts embedded in particular normative orders. Novel border sites are created when these different spheres meet in the daily working lives of posted workers. These borders take a variety of forms, materializing in state and firm borders, and impact the relationship between posted workers and host-country trade unions.

First, national enforcement institutions encounter borders to monitor and/or enforce the rights of posted workers in their sending state. Thus, borders take the form of state borders structured around enforcing labor law within their territory. The inability to monitor and enforce posted workers' rights across borders hinders the effective enforcement of the post-ing rights, rendering posted migrants disproportionately vulnerable to crim-inal victimization and workplace exploitation. Second, subcontracting chains differentiate the rights of workers between firms. Thus, borders take the form of borders between the main and the subcontracting firms[1] that sepa-rate workers from the host-country institutional industrial relations sys-tems. Third, the embeddedness in different normative frames of reference between the trade union and the posted workers, as well as between the host-country orientation of the unions and the home-country orientation of the workers, inhibits meaningful interaction between the two parties. The border thus takes the form of borders to the building of an effective soli-daristic labor force. Interlinking these borders is a useful way of thinking about the shape of the current EU labor market.

The fundamental function of the border is delineation. Borders can delineate territories, cultures, ideas, and activities but also labor markets, work-sites, and work teams. In this sense, borders can be regarded as "institu-tions" governing the extent of inclusion and exclusion between a territorial or membership group and/or groups of workers (Anderson 1992; Cassarino 2006). Scholars conceptualize actors and institutions as being mutually con-stitutive of one another (Jackson 2010). Borders are not static; rather, they are socially constructed (Paasi 1996) through state practices (Berman 2003), through the European Commission (Kostadinova 2013), and by transnational companies, workers, employers, and capital (McGrath-Champ, Herod, and Rainnie 2010; Herod 1998), each with their own concerns. To grasp the vari-ation between different forms of mobile labor in a pan-European labor mar-ket and the rights of mobile workers, it is necessary to examine the creation of borders at the state level and complement this with insights into how bor-ders are constructed in the daily working lives of mobile workers in a pan-European labor market which the chapter will turn to now.

Bordering Practices in Transnational Workspaces

Borders to Regulatory Enforcement

Territorial borders confine a territory and usually an area in which a spe-cific law applies (Del Sarto 2013). They are typically understood as the sites at which the sovereign authority of states to exclude is exercised (Torpey 1998). However, in relation to transnational worker posting, the key claims of states to control exit and entry of labor migrants and enforce labor law within fixed borders are curtailed. In that sense, these borders may exceed the territory of a given polity. The limited sovereignty of EU member states over their labor markets is visible in relation to the detection and enforcement capabilities of national labor inspectors. From a Weberian perspective— whereby the state "upholds monopoly of the legitimate use of physical force" (Weber 1947, 154)—enforcement officers in the German context can be re-garded as agents of state crafting and are therefore a good indication of where the sovereign border lies in the posting relationship.

In Germany, the central agency inspecting labor market standards is the FKS within the customs authorities. This has been the case since the unifica-tion of Germany and can be seen in the context of a more general trend within German law of conceptualizing immigration almost entirely as a labor-control issue (Stobbe 2002). In 1998, the FKS received criminal pros-ecution authority, and the officials were given the status of federal police offi-cers. In addition, the FKS has been given the authority not only to take mea-sures under police law but also to act as an investigator of the public prosecutor's office. This function is associated with additional powers. Most of the work of the officials involves the application of administrative law, but they also fre-quently enforce criminalized immigration law. FKS enforcers have police-like powers, with many wearing uniforms, driving marked cars, or carrying weapons. They have the power to force entry, search persons and premises, confiscate and retain evidence, and arrest without warrant. Enforcing labor standards for posted workers also falls under the tasks of the FKS.

An important task of the FKS is to check the hours worked. Records of working hours have to be kept on every site. The FKS checks the accounts of the company and inspects whether the pay matches the hours worked. However, nationally organized control systems have struggled to adjust to the cross-borders movement of firms with regard to three issues in particu-lar: (1) the detection of malpractices in the host country, (2) the payment of social security contributions in the home country, and (3) the enforcement of fines for transnationally operating companies.

First, in spite of the requirements to provide documents for inspection, according to an FKS representative, the inspectors rarely notice a discrep-ancy (interview with FKS representative, 2013). The difficulty in detecting malpractices and enforcing fines is due to the employment relationship's embeddedness in two national contexts. The FKS suspects that many documents are manipulated while the actual accounting book is kept in the sending country, or the country where the firm has its seat (interview with labor inspector, 2013). To detect malpractices, the FKS would need to investigate whether wage deductions have taken place or whether the correct amount has been paid to the workers. However, in practice, this is almost always impossible because "the investigative power of the labor inspection stops at the German border on the grounds that they have to respect state sovereignty" (interview with community initiative representative, 2012). One administration official said that "the only way to effectively combat fraud is to open the national data base, which has never been done yet because countries are afraid to. Most countries have horrible privacy watch dogs" (interview with administration official, 2013). To gain back sovereignty over the labor market, national administration would effectively need to give up part of its sovereignty in certain administrative areas. The sovereign border here enables practices of rule avoidance to emerge and be upheld, as discussed in chapter 2.

Second, another task of the FKS is to check whether social security contributions are received in the host country. However, it cannot check whether they have been received in the home country. Before sending a posted worker from one member state to the other, the posting firm has to fill out and submit the A1 form. The A1 form proves the worker's registration in the social security system of the home country. It also affirms the payment of the employer's social security contributions according to the worker's wages, which includes the home-country wages. However, the circumvention practice observed is that firms may deduct an untaxed allowance of a maximum of €60 per day. In the receiving country, such deductions cannot legally be made from the minimum wage; an employer pays these on top of the minimum wage. However, firms deduct this amount from the "minimum pay," thereby reducing the sum on which social contributions need to be paid in the sending country. Therefore, social security benefits are only calculated and paid according to the minimum wage level of the sending state (Dälken 2012). This deprives workers of their legitimate social security contributions. This is a typical example of the problems with cross-border enforcement, and there is no control for or enforcement of this practice.

Third, should a malpractice be uncovered and the employer fined, the enforcement of rights conveyed by the PWD still stops at the national frontier. Fines and the exclusion from public procurement provisions have no prohibitive effect, especially because the fines cannot be enforced in the home country (Zentralverband deutsches Baugewerbe 2006). The cooperation with courts and lawyers in the sending countries necessary to enforce fines is basically nonexistent (interview with SOKA-BAU representative, 2013). If the relevant labor inspectorate wants to check whether the registered company operates legitimately in the sending state or whether it is a genuine company, it has to follow the official administrative procedure: in the case of Germany, the respective customs office reports to the regional tax office, which forwards the report to the finance ministry of state, which in turn sends it to the Federal Ministry of Finance. The Federal Ministry of Finance then sends the report to its counterpart in, for example, Poland, which in turn passes it on to the respective institutions. Any answer has to go back the same way (Zentralverband deutsches Baugewerbe 2006). Within the EU, such requests can take up to one year to be processed. Meanwhile, the possibility exists that the company will either deregister from the commercial register and reregister in a different country or register under a different name. As a result, only 15–20 percent of fines are enforced, while 80–85 percent of breaches of the posting of workers regulation remain without consequences (Zentralverband deutsches Baugewerbe 2006). This is not only the case in Germany. For example, only 15 percent of Dutch administrative fines of foreign-based companies are eventually paid (Wagner and Berntsen 2016). A comparative country study reached similar conclusions on the implementation and application of the PWD, demonstrating that fines are rarely imposed in practice and, furthermore, that the fines that have been imposed are rarely enforced either locally or abroad (Van Hoek and Houwerzijl 2011). Fines are no deterrent, particularly because they are rarely enforced across borders.

As the capabilities of the labor inspection to detect malpractices and enforce standards in these transnational workspaces are severely limited, the likelihood of exploitative practices increases, as shown in the previous chapters. And, while a relatively dense institutional framework exists, a public administration official explained the relation between the inability of the labor inspection to detect malpractices and the transnational nature of the workspaces: "We've seen in every [EU] country that the borders have disappeared for the companies, and they have been reinforced for national administrations. And, in essence, with privacy legislation, et cetera, everybody keeps to himself, and it is so easy to commit fraud. And you really must be very unlucky to get caught" (interview with public administration official, 2013).

National borders have not disappeared; in fact, they have made the insider/outsider divide of membership groups even more visible. One official from the labor inspection explained that "the basic idea, 'I would like to carry out a construction service in Germany,' and I say it now with my own words, 'and [I] want to earn as much money as possible,' has become much easier for firms in the EU. Because they do not have to overcome any obstacles anymore. They do not need work permits. That is all gone. In this respect, it has become much easier for the companies" (interview with labor inspection official, 2013). In conjunction with the other types of social and economic exclusion, unequal access to justice also renders irregular migrants disproportionately vulnerable to criminal victimization and workplace exploitation. There clearly is a discrepancy between the rights that have been created for posted workers and the actual ability to use and enforce these rights. This de- and re-territorialization of state borders intersects with the significant transformations of labor markets in Organisation for Economic Co-operation and Development (OECD) countries since the 1970s (Emmenegger et al. 2012). A key change in this process has been the flexibilization and increasing use of atypical employment contracts (King and Rueda 2008), substantially altering the organizational activity of the main contracting firm and differentiating the rights between employees working at the main and subcontracting firms. Furthermore, the increasing use of subcontracting forms another element in excluding posted workers from the collective voice function that could help them clarify and claim their rights.

Firm Borders

Subcontracting arrangements are prevalent in the production process in the construction and meat industries in Germany. Subcontracting is a cost-saving means to exploit differentials between countries, sectors, and workplaces and to increase or decrease production according to need (Flecker and Meil 2010). Outsourced occupations often see a deterioration of working conditions, such as a reduction of wages, work intensification, increased job insecurity, and higher reliance on nonstandard employment (Grimshaw and Rubery 2005; Flecker and Meil 2010; Gautié and Schmitt 2010). Moreover, these processes produce an increased variation of working conditions along value chains, often resulting in people working side by side yet having different employment conditions. The essential dividing line is thus the border of the firm. To put it differently, the shift in the firm border has stark consequences for the employment relations of a worker. The border between the main contractor and the subcontractor implies the differentiation of rights, entitlements, and services provided to different categories of employees depending on their employment at the main or subcontracting firm.

While the use of subcontracting arrangements has increased since the 1990s in Germany more generally (Bosch and Weinkopf 2008), employing posted workers via subcontracting arrangements adds another dimension to the debate, involving the employment of workers embedded in institutional systems other than the German one (Wagner and Lillie 2014). This is manifested not just in the separation between the main firm and subcontractor but also between the work teams.

The main contractor on construction sites or in meat factories usually remains a German company. Posted workers are hired via subcontractors with their base in lower-wage EU countries to fulfill services. The firm border defines which employment and industrial relations context the worker belongs to. The rights and employment relations differ starkly between subcontracted and main-contractor workers. For example, posted workers are excluded from labor market institutions such as codetermination, collective bargaining, and the firm laws of the main contractor in the host country, all of which provide institutionalized voice functions in the host country (Lillie 2010). In practice, this means that the work environment, social security, and taxation of posted workers refer to a country other than where they work.

The borders of the firm have economic as well as social implications. First, workers are employed via subcontractors due to the cost advantage and flexibility for main contractors (interview with management representative, 2012). Subcontractors can offer a competitive price because they pay minimum wages instead of collective agreement wages in the construction sector and home-country wages in the meat sector because of the absence of a statutory minimum wage. The social security contributions are paid according to the home-base country, which are usually lower than Germany's social security contributions. In this sense, both firm and national borders become strategically important for main contractors in employing posted workers.

Moreover, subcontracting out services gives management flexibility in a volatile price market. A management official at a slaughterhouse expanded on this notion:

> In the meat sector, everything is relatively fast moving. You can, for example, change a particular cut in a second by telling the foreman that this is the new specification, and then you have altered the system within minutes. In the meat sector, the price is calculated by weekly rates. This means you make the price with the client on a weekly basis and, at the end of one week, the new price for the next week. Every week, there is a new acquisition price for a pig and the prices for the individual sections, so the price for the processed meat parts has to be adjusted depending on the acquisition price. So, we are faced with relatively short-term price changes. (Interview with management official of slaughterhouse, 2013)

The subcontracting of parts of the meat cutting process is based on the idea of ensuring competitive advantage within a volatile global market. However, one works councilor described this as an ideological mind-set that ensures the continuation of a structure that contributes to the division of the workforce instead of being motivated by cost-saving intentions. "We calculated how much it would cost when the main contractor would hire the subcontracted posted workers for a relatively reasonable, collective bargained wage. The price per kilo would only increase 5% for the end-consumer. The meat is far too cheap. The growth in the '90s and 2000s led to the situation we are in today. Then, the firm needed to hire subcontractors in order to fulfill the demand. This is not the situation anymore today. Now, there is a fictitious divide between the workers that should not be there" (interview with works councilor, 2015). The works councilor referred to the performative act of borders (Paasi 1996) that crosscut between the workforce. Different actors enact and perform the border; such a border may not be simply conceived of as walls, fences, or barricades. Borders here are not physical but the result of the movement of workers and their interactions with other actors (in this case, the subcontractors, works councilor, and the main contracting firm). This is important because, even though the movement across sovereign state borders no longer triggers the notion of a border for EU citizens, the border still exists in the daily lives of citizens and creates a system of differentiated memberships for workers.

Second, workers employed by the main contractor are ensured certain benefits specified in the collective agreements, such as continuous skills-based training, social benefits, and worker interest representation (interview with management official, 2012). The employees at the main company are paid according to collective agreement wages and are represented by works councils. By contrast, posted workers are excluded from the German system of interest representation and voice functions, as discussed in the previous chapters. This isolation substantially increases both the control of the firm over its employees and employee fear of voicing grievances (interview with posted worker, 2012). It is exactly this exclusion materialized at the borders of the firms, wherein posted workers are isolated from voice functions, that makes the claiming of posted workers' rights difficult. Here, borders take the form of borders between the main and the subcontracting firms that separate workers from the host-country institutional industrial relations systems. There are no outlets for voicing grievances in order to achieve socially efficient levels of minimum protection for the workers. Firms are able to profit from the freedom of movement and services by saving on labor costs, but workers are excluded from collective agreement pay, benefits, and voice functions.

Implications of the Spatial Reconfiguration on Solidarity

Trade unions have never been able to represent the interests of all workers equally. History has shown that workers' organizations have always faced the problem of reconciling particularist and universalist interests. Union representation always involves the making of choices. To be effective, unions must "pick their fights," which raises questions about trade union democracy and trade union leaders' capacity to act strategically in a way that advances the interests of most of the union's members or the "working class" in general (Gumbrell-McCormick and Hyman 2013). This has been the case for the working class within "bounded nation states," but diverse national arrangements in the field of industrial relations have integrated the working classes into the nation-state structure (Visser 1996). Despite its internationalist ideology, the history of organized labor is profoundly linked to the nation-state (Erne 2008) and notwithstanding formal declarations of international solidarity, trade unions' dominant frame of reference remains the national arena (Marino 2015). In general, unions have taken the position that posted workers have a right to work in their host countries, but their pay must be in line with local standards. The concern is the protection of the national labor market from social dumping (Cremers 2011; Meardi 2012). Trade unions have an interest in maintaining the norms within the home country because they helped create them in negotiations with the employers. They are also concerned with integrating posted workers into the collective channels of worker representation, such as the previously discussed creation of the EMWU, the establishment of the fair mobility centers, grassroots organizational tactics, or media pressure, so as to change the political landscape. While the lack of resources hinders meaningful interaction between posted workers and the trade unions, the motivations, hopes, and strategies of posted workers may also differ from those of unions. A representative of IG BAU fleshed this idea out:

> The problem is that the people know they should receive €13 here, but, in their home country, they agree to receive a different amount with a handshake. The employer is more or less open about adhering to the German wage norm on paper. Basically, workers contact us when they do not receive the amount they agreed to in the home country. For us, this is, I would say, a motivation problem, because the workers support their own exploitation with these agreements and support social security and tax fraud and related issues. Humanely, I can understand it, but, politically, it is difficult for us because we created the minimum standards for them. (Interview with IG BAU representative, 2011)

Though this may sound like a blatant admission of undercutting the host country's labor standards, it omits the hopes and strategies of posted workers that may have nothing to do with "social dumping." While there may be an implicit bargain involved in paying posted migrants less, this is not because posted workers accept this as a just and fair state of affairs. Contrary to conventional claims, labor migration is not necessarily a purely voluntary process (Cohen 1987). However, most of the interviewed persons signed up for posted work because of socioeconomic problems, particularly unemployment. This leads to accepting practices that may not uphold the normative standards in Germany.

According to a labor inspection officer, this development also impacts the relationship between posted and native workers: "In the past, we detected a strong solidarity between the workers. They would not tell us a thing. If you asked Company A about Company B, which operates on the same site, workers would not react. Over the years, this has been continuously improved—improved from our point of view—because people have realized that they [foreign posted workers] push them out of the market and that, at some point, their job is in danger, so they better tell us something about their co-workers" (interview with labor inspection officer, 2013). These two normative frameworks, consisting of the perspective of the workers and the unions and the native workers, materialize the borders between two work or industrial relations contexts. The predicament is that, while unions are understaffed and lack the resources to effectively mobilize posted workers, the workers themselves also mostly refrain from seeking help from the union because of fear of employer intimidation and retaliation. This results in a catch-22 and creates a border between the union and workers, inhibiting efforts from both sides to transgress it.

The impact of European integration on the territorial structuring of politics and territoriality as a fundamental ordering principle of political life embodied in the modern nation-state is at the heart of the debate in international relations and comparative politics. In this line of inquiry, the borders of and within the EU are recognized as being "permeable" (Kohler-Koch 2005, 13) and increasingly "fuzzy" (Christiansen and Jørgensen 2000, 73). Scholars have described the current state of the EU in relation to territoriality as bearing resemblance to a neomedieval empire (Zielonka 2000) or a "maze" Europe (Christiansen and Jørgensen 2000, 74). The neomedieval concept, particularly in relation to borders, is similar to what Caporaso (1996), Ruggie (1993), and others have identified as a postmodern alternative to the Westphalian form of the state. While the Westphalian system defines the world in territorially bounded spaces, the postmodern model is about unbundling territoriality (Ruggie 1993). Instead of seeing the EU as a new type of Westphalian (federal) state with a central government in charge of a certain territory with clear-cut borders, the neomedieval model describes the EU as a space in which authorities overlap, sovereignty is divided, institutional arrangements are mixed, and citizenship is diversified (Zielonka 2000). In this EU space, the inside/outside line between membership groups is said to be blurred, and borders are recognized as "soft," over time becoming "less territorial, less physical and less visible" (Zielonka 2000, 510). In a similar vein, Christiansen and Jørgensen describe the multiplication of new borders resulting from the dissolution of borders as dividing lines between jurisdictions, which are "perhaps not that significant" (Christiansen and Jørgensen 2000, 68).

Empirical findings of this book have shown that, in relation to the freedom of services and labor mobility, borders are neither soft border zones nor are these discursive/social borders less significant. This chapter argues that, in relation to labor and industrial rights, the borders are indeed significant for EU citizens encountering them. Instead of blurring the inside/outside divide between membership groups, these borders strengthen the divide between mobile posted workers with less pay and fewer rights and native workers with higher pay and better employment rights. The types of borders especially significant for posted workers are the borders for labor market regulation that inhibit the enforcement of labor rights as well as firm borders that separate workers from the host-country institutional industrial relations systems.

In line with the postmodern conception of borders, a salient feature of the borders in relation to transnational posting that this chapter discusses is their markedly porous character. However, while borders in the EU have become porous, it seems that the permeability only goes one way. Bauböck (2015) usefully conceptualizes borders as membranes, which means they should be regarded as stable but at the same time permeable. This is relevant when looking at the structure of the pan-European labor market. Membranes serve as an accurate analogy because the membrane of a cell helps "maintain a difference between the chemical operations occurring inside and outside the cell, but it does so through processes of exchange and transformation of chemical substances. If the membrane sealed off the cell from its biological environment, the cell would die" (Bauböck 2015, 172). A membrane is a selective barrier; it allows some things to pass through but prevents others. The degrees of selectivity of membranes differ. For one, they may be impermeable, not allowing anything to pass through. Furthermore, they may be selectively permeable, allowing only certain things to pass through and blocking others from passing through. They may also be unidirectionally or monodirectionally permeable, allowing things to pass through in only one direction. Finally, they may be omnipermeable, letting anything pass through without selectivity.

The structures in the EU labor market are best understood as unidirectional membranes: the objective of borders is not so much to hamper the free flow of services across jurisdictions in question but rather to open them up to capital while impeding the effective enforcement of workers' employment and social rights. Even though a regulatory system has been created for hypermobile posted workers, it leaves gaps that constrain the ability to enforce or claim workers' rights.

State-centered regimes remain foundational elements of the EU state system. However, the complex regulatory embeddedness of posted workers and the related opaqueness of their employment relationship reduce states' capabilities to regulate within their own territories. Member states can no longer fully enforce order over their defined territory as regards the movement of persons and services. Practices such as double-bookkeeping, with one book in the host country and the other book in the home country, as well as social dumping practices and fines that cannot be traced across borders, create borders to the proper monitoring of the labor rights of posted workers. The border that exists for national administrations opens the door for exploitative practices and the possibility for private actors to strategize around national borders. The importance of the reconfiguration of state borders is therefore interrelated with the institutional reconfiguration of firms.

The current debate over the future of the state and the EU in relation to its borders departs from the vantage points of the state or the supranational levels (Del Sarto 2013; Nadalutti 2013; Kostadinova 2013). However, the shift in state borders intersects with other bordering processes that need to be taken into account in the current discussion. For example, the institutional political economy literature acknowledges that, next to states, nonstate entities—including employers—possess the ability to significantly influence the market economy (Streeck 2009). A case in point is Katzenstein's (1987) analysis of the German industrial relations system constituted by a weak and decentralized state as well as private actors that, in the 1970s and mid-1980s, became partners in cooperative governance. What Katzenstein (1987) described as a "semi-sovereign" state exemplified the influence of private actors in the market economy. For the purposes of this chapter, it is important that the changing strategies of private actors may eventually also affect the effective functioning of the public institutions. In the 1980s and 1990s, "the public use of private organized interests, as described by Katzenstein and others, turned into a private use of the public interest" (Streeck 2003, 4).

In a similar vein, in today's pan-European labor market, because of the significance of nation-state borders in relation to posting, firms strategically "use" and exploit these borders. One consequence of this is that borders are constructed wherever they are needed. Thus, the permeability of firm borders also goes one way: while firms can benefit from low-wage labor through the freedom of movement and services, they are able to exclude workers from in-firm voice functions, added benefits, and skills development by employing them via subcontracting arrangements. Posted workers remain isolated from the institutional and native in-firm employment framework without being included in collective channels of interest representation. Firms now regularly use outsourcing to smaller firms as a way to weaken labor power and avoid works council involvement (Holst 2014).

The added dimension in the sphere of posted work is that the European dimension offers employers additional power resources due to the increasing inability of states to regulate and properly monitor the labor rights of posted workers (Wagner 2015a). Firms use the lack of a strong union presence and the inability of labor inspectorates to enforce the law across borders to create an institutional life of their own in defiance of regulations. This is especially harmful for posted workers because they are oftentimes unaware of their rights and unfamiliar with host-country trade union structures, have no previous experience of collectivism, and are structurally dependent on the employment relationship. Moreover, union power is further diminished by the cross-border nature of the employment relationship. The borders of firms are therefore just as fluid and in need of academic attention as the borders of the state (Martinez Lucio and Mackenzie 2004). By exploiting these strategically, capital is able to remove specific workspaces, contexts, and categories of people from the protection they would normally enjoy within sovereign states (Wagner and Lillie 2014).

The interrelationship of the shifting nature of state and firm borders has significant implications for organized labor in the host country and worker voice of posted workers. While trade unions usually start from an ideological basis of working class solidarity, their actual functioning as organizations is often closely tied to local communities and national identities and developed according to nation-state institutional systems (Erne 2008). Unions are caught in contradictions. Union migration policy has largely been directed toward long-term migration. These strategies have mostly been ineffective with regard to increasingly circular migration patterns. In the face of these problems, German unions have focused on demands for more effective controls. By representing posted work predominantly as a labor supply phenomenon, underlying structural tensions are not adequately addressed. Therefore, the host-country orientation of the unions and the home-country orientation of the workers inhibit meaningful interaction between the two parties, hindering the building of an effective solidaristic labor force. While capital can move effortlessly across state borders, trade unions experience borders in their efforts to represent posted workers and enforce their rights. The isolated situation places posted workers in a precarious position, creating a gray zone in which employer practices fluidly change between legal and illegal practices with a high potential for worker extortion.

While the state border in the posting relationship still has a crucial border function, the case of posted work also sheds light on the fact that borders are not constructed solely by European or national policies but by multiple actors who occupy different positions and have unequal power—firms, labor inspectors, trade unions, works councilors, and posted workers, each following a grid of different strategies and practices. Borders have a performative (Butler 1998) aspect to them in the sense that different actors enact and perform the border. The shifts of borders are based on uneven and unstable resources, and the actors located at the key points of those border shifts, such as trade unions, have not necessarily been constituted in a manner suitable to adapt to these changes. The interrelationship between firm and sovereign territorial spaces allows for new kinds of institutional spaces to emerge, which become less and less attached to the border of the territory but create and reproduce new institutional borders within the territory. These borders are not to be found at the nation-state level but disintegrate into a multiplicity of fragmented borders.

In the case of posting, closed and open borders exist in the same space, curtailing the rights of posted workers and weakening labor power. The examination of the way in which various types of borders make inclusion/ exclusion visible, as well as who is involved in making them visible in a transnational labor market, can have important effects on understandings of and responses to posted work. In that sense, borders do not merely separate; they bring together. They have the potential to be resisted and to create a portal for change (Rumford 2008). It is for this reason that the discussion of the shape of the current European labor market requires an analysis of the form of regulation and the interface between its different sites and actors that create borders; these interactions between sites and actors hint at possible solutions.

Chapter 6

Broadening the Scope

Early in 2008 a story broke that would be discussed in newspapers and political debates in Germany for years to come—a tale familiar to the people from other advanced economies as well: the troubling working conditions of migrant workers, in particular in the successful German meat industry. The radical growth in precarious employment was mainly associated with posted labor migrants who reported excessively long working times, extremely low hourly pay rates, and the poor quality of much of the accommodation made available by the meat processing companies. These conditions have been deplored as the "criminal practices of modern slavery" (Doelfs 2012). Belgium, France, and Austria have accused Germany of unfair competitive practices because posted workers have been employed on dumping wages (EFFAT 2013). Not only trade unions and NGOs but also national and international press reported that the German labor law allowed for a system of institutional exploitation of mobile labor in the meat as well as construction, care work, and truck driving (among other) sectors (Greven 2014).

Academics, media, and policymakers alike asked "how in a country, characterized as a coordinated market economy with strong employers' associations and trade unions, it was possible to create and maintain such a low cost labor market segment" (Wagner and Hassel 2016). According to conventional wisdom, the German political economy is understood to be a coordinated market economy with strong collective representation rights for both labor and capital based on a comprehensive vocational training system (Hall and Soskice 2001). Today, parts of the labor market within the German political economy fall outside of this traditional conception. My intention is that this book lessens the surprise and increases understanding of the persistence of these practices in our contemporary context. In order to do so, this book addressed the largely still-unexplored lived experiences of mobile workers in the pan-European labor market and the regulatory dynamics within transnational workspaces in the EU, where posted work is prevalent. At the end of this book, the reader will, I hope, have learned (1) how and under which conditions the regulatory posting framework is implemented differently at the workplace than at the policy level, (2) the extent to which posted workers are constrained from exercising voice through collective channels of representation in the host country, (3) the conditions under which transnational action can occur, and (4) how firm and state borders interact in a pan-European labor market to create differentiated membership for workers.

One of my intentions was to analyze the enactment and persistence of particular institutional frameworks. Throughout the chapters, I repeatedly noted that the institutions of a political economy can best be understood in relation to how they have been enacted at different levels. Each chapter then investigated which institutional contexts enable and condition the room for the maneuvering of the particular actors involved in the posting process. This book stressed the possible transformative capacity of enaction. It focused on the workplace level, examining actors involved in the posting relationship, including posted workers themselves, as opposed to policymakers. The aim was to portray how local affairs both sustain and prompt shifts in the posting regulatory framework. By illuminating the microlevel, which is not part of the standard repertoire of EU integration research (Radaelli and Pasquier 2006), or, indeed, of much of today's institutionalist political economy literature (Streeck 2009), the book aimed to highlight the overall importance of this approach for a dynamic research agenda of European integration and the changing nature of employment relations such an agenda induces. Findings shed additional information on the uneven and multilevel dynamics of EU integration and the discrepancy between market making and social integration.

This qualitative case study and the in-depth interview data with posted workers, trade unionists, NGOs, works councilors, management, labor inspectors, and policymakers support four main findings. First, transnational subcontracting allows the emergence of different regulatory spaces at the national and workplace levels. Second, it opens up exit options for capital but constrains voice options for unions, works councils, and mobile workers. Third, transnational workspaces create opportunities for transnational action; however, these opportunities take on other forms than is usually expected within the German political economy. Fourth, it is necessary to analyze how different kinds of borders—in this case, state and firm borders—intersect in order to fully grasp the structure of a pan-European labor market.

These broad findings reflect the discussions within the respective chapters. Chapter 2 showed how the pan-European labor market opens up exit options for capital but isolates posted workers from collective channels of worker representation. The chapter related the changes in labor market regulation to changes in the nature and organization of the nation-state. These findings contribute to comparative institutional analysis by highlighting how the de-territorialization of previously "bounded" institutional, political, economic, or industrial relations systems decreases collective voice and increases institutional exit.

Chapter 3 studied how firms creatively enact the posting framework. It examined how these mechanisms initiate a process of institutional change through power dynamics at the microlevel relevant for theories on institutional change generally. The findings show that the possibility for firms to diverge from rules is accelerated in a transnational setting. This is due not only to the prevalence of unequal power dynamics between firms and workers but also to the inability to publicly or collectively enforce rules. The examination of how actors engage with this transnational institution contributes to institutional theory by bridging the gap between institutional context and its appropriation by firms, posted workers, and unions.

Chapter 4 explored the conditions for posted worker resistance. It high-lighted the shift in strategy of the German meat sector union to form coalitions with community organizations to mobilize posted workers. It demonstrated the conditions under which such coalitions emerge and are successful, such as a lack of union power and resources, a useful division of work, and a media strategy focusing on social justice. It contributes to blind spots in cross-national comparative perspectives based on institutional equilibrium and sectors with union strongholds. It emphasized the impor-tance of engaging with migration and its configurations in different indus-trial relations systems, an area of study too often neglected by industrial relations scholars.

Chapter 5 considered how the changing nature of state and firm borders affects posted workers in transnational workspaces. The insights of three key areas of study—the changing nature of state borders, institutional analy-sis, and the industrial relations literature on transnational solidarity—were combined to develop an original framework that enhances both our theo-retical and practical understandings of transnational workspaces in the EU. The chapter contributes to the literature on European integration and the territorial structuring of politics. A bottom-up approach was imple-mented that aimed to enhance the understanding of how the debordering of a political territorial space affects the European labor market and its mobile workers, which is largely missing from the debate (Meardi 2012).

All chapters pointed to the weakening of labor power and labor market regulation due to the disembedding of labor relations from the territorial nation-state. In establishing the freedom to provide services, the EU created a European economic space but has not carved out spaces for controls. These examples hint at the fact that migration and mobility, since the enlargement of the EU, have been accompanied by the emergence of new forms of in-equality. These examples do not merely contradict the official rhetoric, ac-cording to which internal mobility in the EU contributes to a wealthier and more prosperous Europe (Kahanec and Zimmermann 2009); they also indi-cate that there is a fundamental difference between the experiences of EU citizens and those of non-EU citizens, because the latter group faces consid-erably greater restrictions and limitations to mobility than the former (Bigo 2009; Tsoukala 2005), which does not stop in either the meat and construc-tion industries or in Germany.

Regulatory Arbitrage across Sectors

Posting is most prominent in the construction and meat industries in Germany but has expanded to other industries since 2004. However, the rights of other mobile workers, such as temporary agency workers or self-employed labor migrants, are also being circumvented in other industries where such employment channels are more common. In sectors such as cleaning, logistics, care work, and industrial services, employees with flexible employment relations originating mainly from eastern European countries are increasingly replacing "core" employees (Dälken 2012). Labor migrants are also increasingly being employed in various sectors (such as the shipping trade) and in winter services. The reasons their rights are being circumvented are similar to the findings in this book: labor migrants in flexible employment relationships have little bargaining power and are largely isolated to the German institutional system of interest representation within which they lack judicial coverage (Dälken 2012). The different sectoral minimum wages in Germany create confusion for employees and complicate effective controls for the labor inspection authorities.

One sector that more specifically illustrates the underlying reasons firms employ or do not employ labor migrants or posted workers is Amazon and its distribution centers. Amazon.com is one of the biggest online retailers operating worldwide. To be able to meet the demands of a growing online market, the company is constantly opening new sites and relocating distribution warehouses and logistic centers around the world. Decisions on location are guided by available infrastructure accessibility of markets (interview with ver.di representative, 2013). Distribution centers can be found in France, Germany, Italy, Spain, and the UK. Amazon has opened new locations in the Czech Republic and Poland. The sites are often located close to Amazon's main markets in Germany or the UK. Amazon warehouses have a high need for personnel, but in many cases, such as the Bad Hersfeld distribution center in Germany, only a small part of the workforce is recruited from the local labor market. Temporary mobile workers from all over Europe (in particular from Spain, Hungary, Romania, and Poland) are recruited during peak seasons (the Christmas and Easter periods) to cover high staff requirements. During these periods, Amazon relies on temporary agency firms to provide enough suitable workers on time. Thus, numerous temporary foreign workers and national temporary workers are recruited (interview with ver.di representative, 2013).

Another industry in which the influx and precarious labor market conditions of posted workers are present is shipbuilding. In 2013, two Romanian posted workers who worked at the Meyer shipyard died in a mass housing fire. As a consequence, the Meyer shipyard was accused of exploiting workers because the fire was a result of the precarious housing situation. An agreement between IG Metall and the Meyer Werft was intended to strengthen workers' rights while preserving the controversial contracts for posted work as an instrument. The collective agreement covered the employment conditions of employees working at subcontracting firms and contained information, control, and participation rights for the works council in the outsourcing process. It obliged subcontracting firms to adhere to standards related to working hours, health and safety, and adequate housing as well as a minimum wage of €8.50 per hour. A permanent working group consisting of a works council and management controlled the implementation and consulted about the cancellation of a contractual relation, and, in the case of a disagreement about the scope of the subcontracts, the in-firm arbitration committee could be consulted. The Meyer shipyard also committed itself to inform and consult with the works council in detail about its subcontracting relations. If the works council demanded, it could look into the contracts as well as the nature and scope of service work of the subcontractors.

In sectors where hardly any posted workers are present, such as the German metal or telecommunications industries, we nevertheless see a trend toward outsourcing. The employment relations in such contexts, at least to a certain extent, have commonalities with those of posted workers. Evidence from metalworking and telecommunications suggests that a fragmented landscape of labor relations exists in Germany (Benassi and Dorigatti 2015; Doellgast 2009). In fact, German labor relations have undergone a significant reconstruction in the past few decades. The bargaining coverage is decreasing, workplaces without codetermination are expanding, and nonstandard employment is proliferating (Bosch and Weinkopf 2008). As a consequence, the core institutions of labor relations are losing their previous inclusiveness. Until the late 1980s, sector agreements covered the vast majority of workplaces, firm-level codetermination was widespread, and statutory provisions such as dismissal protection and sick pay left virtually the entire workforce shielded. Due to the legal-political institutions' inclusiveness, labor relations contributed to the decommodification of labor, a characteristic of the German model of postwar organized capitalism (Streeck 2009). The ongoing decline of institutional inclusiveness resulted in a tangible recommodification of labor and increasing poverty risks among the lower ranks of the labor force (Dörre 2005b). As a result, even in the allegedly stable core areas, the institutions of labor relations have gradually been transformed from market-constituting institutions to market-dependent variables. Vertical disintegration has played an important role in this process of institutional commodification. It has not only moved the core-periphery boundary; it has also been deployed to subjugate collective bargaining, workplace codetermination, and the utilization of labor laws to firm-level economic calculations (Holst 2014). The processes of labor market dualization within and across national economies both are part of and signal the variegated nature of regulatory configurations in European political economies (Brenner, Peck, and Theodore 2010). These examples point to an "in-between" space in which workers become borderline citizens not only down subcontracting chains within the national economy but also in transnational workspaces.

Borderline Labor in Different Contexts and Countries

This book has discussed alternative, uneven, and extremely dynamic forms of regulation beyond a self-contained view of the national level that do not per se undermine the nation-state. In these spaces, differentiated forms of regulation are pertinent insomuch as the regular institutional system largely does not apply to them. This is similar to what Ong (2006) labels "neoliberalism as exception," Agnew (2009) depicts as "portable sovereignty," and Lillie (2010), drawing on Palan (2003), labels "spaces of exception." These authors depict spaces in which sovereignty is fragmented and in which firms can strategize around this disjointed regulation. Palan (2003) explained this as a process in which social and political controls are selectively not enforced to allow capital a freer hand in designing the social relations of production. The main concern in this book is not to accept the "lack of regulation" per se but to investigate how these spaces are structured and how actors in these spaces engage with the institutional framework in place. If one seeks to understand how these spaces come into being and are sustained, one must look not only at the structures laid down by laws and authorities but also at the various agents reconstituting those structures.

This approach may produce important insights for other industries or policy fields in the EU or other parts of the world where processes of de-territorialization interact with the changing nature of employment relations. Rather than being an exclusively German problem, dangerous working conditions and precarious work, particularly in the context of increasing subcontracted (external) labor, have been reported in the construction, meat, care, and distribution industries (among others) across Europe (Hamann 2010), as well as in Southeast Asia (Shire et. al. 2018; Altreiter, Fibich, and Flecker 2015) and the United States.

In the EU, similar processes occur in industries such as shipbuilding (Wagner and Lillie 2014), warehouse distribution (Berntsen 2016), and trucking. The labor markets of these industries are in the process of being transformed. While this book focuses on the German setting, other studies have shown that various EU countries have struggled to adapt their labor market policies to implement the PWD (for an overview, see Kall and Lillie 2017). For example, Lillie and Greer (2007) looked at transnational posted work in the construction industry in Germany, Finland, and the UK and examined how transnational politics and labor markets undermine national industrial relations systems in Europe. Moreover, Lillie, Wagner, and Berntsen (2014) have discussed the similarities of construction firms in Germany, the Netherlands, and Finland in evading or altering the application of regulation in their employment relations. This cross-country comparison found that construction firms oftentimes claim they are complying with the host country's rules and the PWD, but these claims are difficult to check, and the firms may in fact be violating their home country's regulations. Employer behavior in the countries examined was fairly similar and made possible by the ambiguous rule system surrounding posted workers and their work environments.

Changing Regulations, Changing Practices?

In response to the loophole between posted workers' established rights and their appropriation in practice, what are the implications of these findings for institutional reforms to the worker-posting framework at the national and EU levels? One significant change in the regulation of posted work occurred in the summer of 2014 in the German meat industry. In July 2014, the four largest meat processing companies reacted to the immense media pressure on worker exploitation in the meat industry and pledged to end precarious employment practices for posted workers. The main vehicle to do this was to stop employing workers via posting contracts but to employ the same workers via a subcontractor with its seat in Germany. Within a year's time, all previously employed posted workers should find themselves in an employment relationship with a German employer and, as a result, receive minimum pay and health benefits accordingly, and be provided with proper accommodation. This pledge was formalized in the voluntary commitment of the meat industry (six signatories at the time but now eighteen meat companies). This agreement promised to (1) improve working and living conditions for employees in the meat processing industry, (2) adapt the organizational structures by July 2016 in such a way that all workers deployed in their plants will be in a regular employment relationship, registered in Germany, and liable for social insurance contributions (this amounts to *abandoning the use of posted workers*, whose social insurance contributions and entitlements are determined by the usually considerably lower standards prevailing in their home countries), (3) increase and further develop the share of their *core workforce*, and (4) provide *training* places and put in place the appropriate promotional and recruitment measures to ensure they are filled.

Three of the large slaughterhouses in Germany either stopped or significantly scaled down the usage of posting contracts by July 2016 and from then on concluded subcontracts with German firms or German subsidiaries of foreign companies only (interview with works councilors slaughterhouse, 2016). Employing migrant workers at subcontractors with the home base in Germany, instead of abroad, implies that these workers are employed according to the German social insurance law, which is usually higher and more easily accessible than the equivalent in a lower wage sending country. Companies also committed themselves to increase the proportion of core workers. The positive outcomes of this are that workers have better access to healthcare services and better legal enforcement of their rights because the rights framework is within the host-country framework. Moreover, the federal government adopted the law on securing workers' rights in the meat processing industry. The concrete results of this law will have to be evaluated at a later stage.

However, there are still considerable gaps in both collective representation (weak organization on both the employers' and the employees' sides, small number of collective agreements, and only a few works councils) and enforcement of labor standards in the industry. Even though posted workers are employed at a company based in Germany, they are employed by subcontractors nonetheless and employee representatives continually report unlawful practices such as wage deductions for knives and clothing.

The research findings call for several further improvements. First, binding targets for the reduction in posted work contracts should be established. Second, there should be a binding target to increase the percentage of core workers. Third, codetermination rights for works councilors should be improved. Fourth, collective redress should be possible, and fifth, the burden of proof in cases of bogus subcontracting should be reversed.

At the European level, the latest policy initiation calls for a revision of the Posting of Workers Directive itself. The revision aims to remunerate posted workers in accordance with host member state law and practices and make collective agreements universally applicable to posted workers across all sectors. At the time of writing, the revision is being discussed at the committee level in the European Parliament. The most recent adopted policy relating to posted work is the Enforcement Directive, which addresses concerns about better enforcing the rules laid out in the Posting of Workers Directive. The final document was passed just before the European Parliamentary election in 2014. One of the most contentious issues of the ED is the specification regarding which rights apply when the worker is deemed as falling outside the posting framework. As set out in the operationalization of posted work for this book (see the introduction), a fluid labor market has emerged in which it is difficult to disentangle under which rights framework a worker is actually employed. For example, it is often unclear whether the worker de facto falls under the free movement of persons or services (the added complication being if the person is employed via a subcontractor or agency contract) or is unconsciously and bogusly self-employed. Most of the workers interviewed for this book were recruited for the purposes of the posting relationship. They would therefore fall outside the scope of the posting framework. Trade unions demanded a clear definition regarding which law would apply to a worker who is under a de facto but not a de jure posted employment relationship (such as bogusly self-employed workers). The demand was for the ED to clearly state that, in the aforementioned case, the worker would be covered by the entire legislation of the host country. However, the ED does not state which framework would apply and therefore leaves the possibility open to be the country-of-origin framework.[1] The danger here is the introduction of the country-of-origin principle through the back door. The way the posting framework is enacted will thus not be curtailed but may turn out to be justifiable with this legal loophole in place.

This book has argued that this particularly precarious situation for posted workers has evolved due to the discrepancy between nationally embedded regulatory institutions and labor power and the transnational labor market. The ED hardly introduced remedies in this regard. Interestingly, the heated debate in relation to the ED revolved around strengthening the national control measures instead of transnational cooperation. For example, the main debate focused on subcontracting-chain liability and other particular control measures. Social partners of several EU countries pushed for a main-contractor liability for all the elements in the subcontracting chain. According to Article 12 of the ED, only the direct subcontractor can be held liable. It is left to the member state to determine the exact tool to enforce such abuse in the subcontracting chain. Paradoxically, the ED leaves room for the member states to decide relevant enforcement measures while simultaneously repeatedly cautioning that additional measures need to be "justified" and "proportionate."

For example, national inspectorates are not restricted in imposing particular measures. However, any additional measures have to be "justified" and "proportionate" to avoid creating a barrier or an obstacle to the free provision of services. In fact, throughout the ED, the attention to "proportionate" measures cautions member states to maximize their own tools to avoid infringement procedures. Moreover, the European Commission emphasizes in Article 9 that it will monitor whether the ED is effectively translated into national law. Even though the European Commission has an institutional duty to monitor compliance, this responsibility is usually not written into directives. This draws attention to the importance of employing proportionate instruments at the national level. This may render national regulatory frameworks impotent to counter transnational exploitative practices, as observed in the case of transnational workspaces.

In certain aspects, the ED did advance transnational administrative cooperation. It sets time limits by which authorities of other member states have to respond to requests for assistance (e.g., a two-working-day limit to respond to urgent requests and a 25-working-day limit for nonurgent requests). However, how the actual collection of fines is to be achieved is unresolved. Fines imposed on a posting firm cannot be executed effectively because they are based in a different jurisdiction. Moreover, Article 18 (1) introduces a right for the service providers to contest the fine, penalty, and/or underlying claim. If such a dispute arises, the cross-border enforcement procedure of the fine or penalty imposed will be suspended pending the decision of the appropriate national authority on the matter. Companies making a business model out of worker posting may be able to use this provision as a tool to postpone real execution. In this sense, companies are still able to profit and can strategize around the fact that they are registered in another jurisdiction.

Essentially, the ED barely tackles the underlying structural issues. This book has observed a functional change in the institutional framework. Even though policymakers wanted to remove loopholes, the actual policy framework has not changed much at the EU level. Campbell (2009) argues that most researchers would agree that changes in rules would qualify as instances of institutional change; by contrast, functional changes would not. However, the complexity of the posting regulation and the outcome of the ED demonstrate that highly politicized controversies impede on changing the actual rules of the game through the political process. The heterogeneity of economic interests for both member states and trade unions largely inhibits effective change. These policy struggles more often than not result in vague and ambiguous formulations of legal text that leave wide room for reinterpretation. Therefore, this book points to the importance of paying equal attention to functional change. In light of these rather grim conclusions and policy developments, what, then, are the implications of this research to generate more effective strategies to strengthen workers' rights in transnational workspaces?

What Is to Be Done?

Interested parties in the posting policy field have developed several practical policy recommendations. First, at the national level, trade unions demand the curtailing of the development of long subcontracting chains as a preventive measure against possible abusive practices. Second, there is public demand to significantly upgrade sanctions for noncomplying firms to disincentivize rule circumvention. Third, in Germany, there are proposals to establish a (currently nonexistent) system of legal collective redress. Collective redress enables trade unions to file court proceedings on behalf of workers. Posted workers could file legal proceedings without having to reveal their identities and, thus, protect their employment relationship. Collective redress would give a voice to posted workers' concerns as well as uncover malpractices. Fourth, trade unions demand a formal role in the labor-inspection process, both in its design and in the labor inspections themselves. This may strengthen worker voice as well as enforcement and could include the involvement of social partners such as trade unions.

A European Parliament (2013b) report suggests a transnational measure to strengthen effective enforcement of mobile labor rights. First, the report suggests the introduction of a European agency to handle all kinds of cross-border matters within the field of labor inspections with the aim of more effective administrative cooperation. This could, for example, cover the control of transnational service and letterbox companies, as well as the organization of cross-border controls (European Parliament 2013b). Second, members of European Parliament proposed the implementation of a European social security card, where necessary data such as working time or social security contributions are stored. This would permit labor inspectors to review all the necessary data on the spot. Such a card has already been implemented in the Swedish construction sector and has proved to be an effective way to control workplaces and facilities (European Parliament 2013b). Inspectors would be able to read the information on the cards via detectors. Third, the establishment of an EU-wide register of the A1 form is needed to make controls effective in nation-states and also to quantify the numbers for policy pressure purposes and effective quantitative research.

Apart from these isolated measures, and to move away from the shortcomings of and failures to improve the PWD, it may be progressive to introduce a whole new directive altogether. This directive would focus on and refer to all kinds of cross-border labor mobility in the EU, removing the competition created by different forms of mobility. Such a directive, geared toward a mobile low-wage sector in a pan-European labor market, would articulate and fuse the rights between atypical, posted, and agency work.

Future Research

New EU directives confirm the trend in changing borders between political economic territories and employment relations. For example, the intra-corporate transfer directive (European Parliament and the Council 2013) on conditions of entry and residence of third-country nationals in the framework of an intra-corporate transfer is such an example. "Intra-corporate transfer" means the temporary secondment of a third-country national from an undertaking established outside the territory of a member state and to which the third-country national will return. The directive enables third-country nationals to be posted within the European Single Market. The condition is that they have to have worked for six months within an EU member state in a daughter undertaking of the company for which they normally work. For example, a Russian undertaking can send his employee for a secondment to Poland. The worker could be posted under the PWD to Germany if he or she has worked for the daughter undertaking in Poland for six months. In light of the findings of this book, difficulties in enforcing the regulatory framework in such a situation can easily be imagined.

These findings confirm that similar processes are occurring in other EU member states and in similar policy fields. A similarly complex policy field is the one of portable social rights for intra-EU migrant workers. In theory, every EU citizen has equal right to these social security institutions as long as they are employed. This right should be accessible, moreover, not just in their country of origin but across all member states. Whether this is true in practice, however, is another question. EU citizenship grants extensive rights to remain, work, transfer, and draw social benefits in other member states to those who fall within the status of "worker." However, the answers to the questions "What is work?" and "Who is a worker?" are not straightforward. For example, EU migrants can draw on unemployment benefits if they can show that they have exercised "genuine and effective work" or if they have a "genuine chance of being engaged." Ambiguous legal definitions leave the final decision of access to the interaction between EU migrant workers and administrators. The case of Brexit shows that this is not purely a technical issue and that there are political forces behind benefit denials, gaps, and expulsions (Danaj and Wagner 2016). There are discrepancies between how "work" or "worker" is defined among EU member states. Access to social protection for intra-EU migrant workers is also dependent on the type of work contract. For precariously employed intra-EU migrants, this can mean a de facto exclusion from the social protections of the host state, illuminating differences between how policy is designed and how it is practiced. Here, intra-EU labor migrants are in an in-between position similar to that of posted workers.

Moreover, future research may also look more closely at similar processes within other world regions. Preliminary research comparing labor mobility via services between the EU and Southeast Asia suggests that posted work, or forms comparable to posted work, is increasingly used as an employment flexibilization measure in East Asia (Wagner and Shire 2018). Despite the absence of similar supranational regional regulations, the regional integration of transformation market economies (e.g., China, India, and Vietnam), as well as the well-developed cross-national capacities of the Japanese temporary-staffing industry in East Asia (Coe, Johns, and Ward 2012), indicates developments that parallel some of the driving forces for the expansion of migrant agency work in Europe.

Finally, it is crucial to further investigate the impact of mobility practices on society at large. The politics of differentiation between mobile workers themselves and between mobile workers and native workers has a strong influence on stability in the process of EU integration. Perceived or existing levels of inequality can spur an anti-EU backlash (Burgoon 2013). The Brexit decision, as well as increasing support for populist parties, points to rising levels of xenophobia. EU citizens in several member states have expressed concerns about widening integration. Populist discussions accuse labor migrants of either being "welfare tourists" or of contributing to rising unemployment (Danaj and Wagner, 2016). The Dutch Freedom Party established a website in which it was possible to name and shame eastern European workers who allegedly 'stole' the jobs of native workers. Even though states opened the borders to free mobility via services, many borders remain and are even reinforced in the process of European integration. Drawing attention to the borders that intra-EU migrants encounter may pave the way to re-embed mobile workers into structures of social inclusion and collective resistance. Looking at policy from the migrant perspective can thus show how actors order and utilize regulation within transnational workspaces.

The findings of this book are a snapshot of a particular time and place as well as part of a dynamic process of how policy unfolds in complex settings. As much as supranational policy influences the structures of national and local policy, so should the everyday experience of mobile EU citizens influence the redesign of policy and theory.

Appendix I

Article 3 of the Posting of Workers Directive

Article 3 (1)[1] lists the terms and conditions of employment for posted workers:

Member states shall ensure that, whatever the law applicable to the employment relationship, the undertakings referred to in Article 1 (1) guarantee workers posted to their territory the terms and conditions of employment covering the following matters which, in the member state where the work is carried out, are laid down:

—by law, regulation or administrative provision, and/or
—by collective agreements or arbitration awards which have been declared universally applicable within the meaning of paragraph 8, insofar as they concern the activities referred to in the Annex:

(a) maximum work periods and minimum rest periods;
(b) minimum paid annual holidays;

(c) the minimum rates of pay, including overtime rates; this point does not apply to supplementary occupational retirement pension schemes;[2]

(d) the conditions of hiring-out of workers, in particular the supply of workers by temporary Employment undertakings;

(e) health, safety and hygiene at work;

(f) protective measures with regard to the terms and conditions of employment of pregnant women or women who have recently given birth, of children and of young people;

(g) equality of treatment between men and women and other provisions on non-discrimination.

These minimum requirements in force in the host country "shall not prevent application of terms and conditions of employment which are more favorable to workers" (Article 3(1)).

Appendix II

OVERVIEW OF INTERVIEWS

Overview of Interviews I

Germany	Construction Industry (Number of Interviews)	Meat Industry (Number of Interviews)
Management representative	4	3
Works council representative	4	4
Trade union representative	11	5
Posted workers	28	21
Native workers	4	3
NGO representative	2	4
Participant observation trade union/NGO mobilizing activities	4	4
Total	57	44

These interviews were supplemented with interviews from other relevant actors to contextualize the developments in the construction and meat industries in relation to other sectors as well as to trace relevant policy developments in relation to posting.

Overview of Interviews II

Institution	Number of Interviews
IG Metall representative	2
ver.di representative	4
DGB representative	1
Labor Inspection (FKS) official	2
European Commission official	1
Total	10

Notes

Introduction

1. The term "borderline citizen" was previously used by Studer (2001) and Gleadle (2009) in the context of respectively discussing the relationship between marriage, rules, and citizenship in Switzerland, and analyzing the state of British women as political actors in the early nineteenth century.

2. Article 1.3 (a) (b) (c). For the entire Article 3 of the PWD, see Appendix I.

3. At the time of writing.

4. In a similar vein, in the *Rüffert* case (Case C-346/06), the ECJ ruled that the Public Procurement Act of the German state Lower Saxony, according to which public authorities are obliged to only contract firms if they pay the wages laid down in the relevant sectoral collective agreement, restricted the provision of services in the host member state, and, thus, by extending the *minimum* conditions as established in the PWD, posed a threat to competitiveness in the single market.

2. Posted Work and Transnational Workspaces in Germany

1. In 2004, Cyprus, Czech Republic, Estonia, Hungary, Latvia, Lithuania, Malta, Poland, Slovakia, and Slovenia joined the EU, followed by Bulgaria and Romania in 2007.

3. Management Strategies in Transnational Workspaces

A different version of this chapter was previously published in the *British Journal of Industrial Relations* (see Wagner 2015b).

1. In Germany, the institution that has the task of enforcing, for example, the minimum wage (tasks that in other countries are situated at the labor inspection) is embedded in the institution that literally translates as the "black economy unit" within the customs ministry. For simplicity, I will refer to it as the labor inspection, or FKS, throughout the text. The exact tasks of the FKS are explained further in chapter 5.

4. Posted Worker Voice and Transnational Action

A different version of this chapter was previously published in *Transfer* (see Wagner 2015c).

1. One-euro jobs are intended for unemployed persons to reintegrate into the employment relation. It has been observed that firms use them to employ low-wage labor (Dörre 2005a).

5. Borders in a European Labor Market

A different version of this chapter was previously published in the *Journal of Common Market Studies* (see Wagner 2015a).

1. "Firm borders" is used to describe these borders in the remainder of this chapter. This should not be confused with "firm" borders as in the adjective "firm."

6. Broadening the Scope

1. Recital 11 states: "Where there is no genuine posting situation and a conflict of law arises, due regard should be given to the provisions of Regulation (EC) No 593/2008 of the European Parliament and of the Council ('Rome I') or the Rome Convention that are aimed at ensuring that employees should not be deprived of the protection afforded to them by provisions which cannot be derogated from by an agreement or which can only be derogated from to their benefit. Member States should ensure that provisions are in place to adequately protect workers who are not genuinely posted" (Directive 2014/67 EU).

Appendix I

1. EU Directive 96/71/EC of the European Parliament and the Council of 16 December 1996 concerning the posting of workers in the framework of the provision of services.

2. For the purposes of this directive, the concept of minimum rates of pay referred to in paragraph 1 (c) is defined by the national law and/or practice of the member state to whose territory the worker is posted.

References

Aberbach, Joel D., and Bert A. Rockmann. 2002. "Conducting and Coding Elite Interviews." *Political Science and Politics* 35 (4): 673–76.

Adamson, Fiona, and Madeleine Demetriou. 2007. "Remapping the Boundaries of 'State' and 'National Identity': Incorporating Diasporas into IR Theorizing." *European Journal of International Relations* 13 (4): 489–526.

Afonso, Alexandre. 2012. "Employer Strategies, Cross-Class Coalitions and the Free Movement of Labour in the Enlarged European Union." *Socio-Economic Review* 10 (4): 705–30.

Agnew, John. 2009. *Globalization and Sovereignty*. Plymouth, MA: Rowman and Littlefield.

Ahlberg, Kerstin, Niklas Bruun, and Jonas Malmberg. 2006. "The *Vaxholm* Case from a Swedish and European Perspective." *Transfer: European Review of Labour and Research* 12 (2): 155–66.

Alberti, Gabriella, Jane Holgate, and Maite Tapia. 2013. "Organising Migrants as Workers or as Migrant Workers? Intersectionality, Trade Unions and Precarious Work." *International Journal of Human Resource Management* 24 (22): 4132–48.

Alho, Rolle. 2013. "Varieties of Capitalism and Translocal Linkages Shaping Trade Union Strategy in the Context of Transnational Labour Mobility." *Nordic Journal of Working Life Studies* 3 (3): 133–53.

Almeida, Paul, and Lina Brewster Stearns. 1998. "Political Opportunities and Local Grassroots Environmental Movements: The Case of Minamata." *Social Problems* 45 (1): 37–60.

Alsos, Kristin, and Line Eldring. 2008. "Labour Mobility and Wage Dumping: The Case of Norway." *European Journal of Industrial Relations* 14 (4): 441–59.

Altreiter, Carina, Theresa Fibich, and Jörg Flecker. 2015. "Capital and Labour on the Move. Dynamics of Double Transnational Mobility." In *The Outsourcing Challenge: Organizing Workers across Fragmented Production Networks*, edited by Jan Drahokoupil, 67–87. Brussels: European Trade Union Institute.

Anderson, Bridget. 1992. "The New World Disorder." *New Left Review* 193 (1): 3–13.

Arnholtz, Jens. 2013. "A 'Legal Revolution' in the European Field of Posting? Narratives of Uncertainty, Politics and Extraordinary Events." PhD diss., University of Copenhagen.

Artus, Ingrid. 2014. "Mitbestimmung und Leiharbeit" [Co-determination and fixed term work]. *WSI-Mitteilungen* 67 (2): 113–21.

BA (Bundesagentur für Arbeit). 2015. Beschäftigungsstatistik, Anzahl der Betriebe und sozialversicherungspflichtig Beschäftigten nach Betriebsgrößenklassen in West- und Ostdeutschland in den Jahren 1999–2014, Nürnberg [Employment statistic, number of businesses and social insurance employees according to business size in West and East Germany from 1999–2014]. In author's possession.

BA (Bundesagentur für Arbeit). 2016. Arbeitsmarkt in Zahlen. Sozialversicherungspflichtig und geringfügig Beschäftigte nach Wirtschaftszweigen der WZ 2008 und ausgewählten [Labor market in numbers. Social insurance employees and marginally employed according to industry (WZ 2008 and selected characteristics)], Merkmalen, Nürnberg. In author's possession.

Baccaro, Luccio, Robert Boyer, Colin Crouch, Marino Regini, Paul Marginson, Richard Hyman, Rebecca Gumbrell-McCormick, and Ruth Milkman. 2010. "Discussion Forum I: Labour and the Global Financial Crisis." *Socioeconomic Review* 8 (2): 341–76.

Baccaro, Luccio, Kerstin Hamann, and Lowell Turner. 2003. "The Politics of Labour Movement Revitalization: The Need for a Revitalized Perspective." *European Journal of Industrial Relations* 9 (1): 119–33.

Bailey, David. 2010. "The European Rescue, Recommodification, and/or Reterritorialisation of the (Becoming-Capitalist) State? Marx, Deleuze, Guattari, and the European Union." *Journal of International Relations and Development* 13 (4): 325–53.

Bamber, Greg J., Russell D. Lansbury, and Nick Wailes. 2011. *International and Comparative Employment Relations*. 5th ed. London: SAGE.

Barnard, Catherine. 2008. "Viking and Laval: An Introduction." In *The Cambridge Yearbook of European Legal Studies*, vol. 10, edited by Catherine Barnard, 463–92. Oxford: Hart.

Barnard, Catherine. 2009. "'British Jobs for British Workers': The Lindsey Oil Refiners Dispute and the Future of Local Labour Clauses in an Integrated EU Market." *Industrial Law Journal* 38 (3): 245–77.

Barnes, Jeb. 2008. "Courts and the Puzzle of Institutional Stability and Change: Administrative Drift and Judicial Innovation in the Case of Asbestos." *Political Research Quarterly* 61 (4): 636–48.

Batt, Rosemary, D. Holman, and U. Holtgrewe. 2009. "The Globalization of Service Work: Comparative Institutional Perspectives on Call Centers." *Industrial & Labor Relations Review* 62 (4): 453–88.

Bauböck, Rainer. 2015. "Rethinking Borders as Membranes." In *Rethinking Border Control for a Globalizing World*, edited by Leanne Weber, 169–78. London: Routledge.

Behrens, Martin, and Andreas Pekarek. 2012. "To Merge or Not to Merge? The Impact of Union Merger Decisions on Workers' Representation in Germany." *Industrial Relations Journal* 43 (6): 527–47.

Benassi, Chiara, and Lisa Dorigatti. 2015. "Straight to the Core—Explaining Union Responses to the Casualization of Work: The IG Metall Campaign for Agency Workers." *British Journal of Industrial Relations* 53 (3): 533–55.

Bengtsson, Erik. 2013. "Swedish Trade Unions and European Union Migrant Workers." *Journal of Industrial Relations* 55 (2): 174–89.

Benkhoff, Birgit, and Vicky Hermet. 2008. "Zur Verbreitung und Ausgestaltung geringfügiger Beschäftigung im Einzelhandel. Eine explorative Studie aus der Perspektive von Management und Beschäftigten" [On the dissemination and design of marginal employment in the retail sector. An explorative study from the perspective of management and employees]. *Industrielle Beziehungen* 15 (1): 5–31.

Berman, Jaqueline. 2003. "(Un)Popular Strangers and Crises (Un)Bounded: Discourses of Sex-Trafficking, the European Political Community and the Panicked State of the Modern State." *European Journal of International Relations* 9 (1): 37–86.

Berntsen, Lisa. 2015. "Stepping Up to Strike: A Union Mobilization Case Study of Polish Temporary Agency Workers in the Netherlands." *Transfer: European Review of Labour and Research* 21 (4): 399–412.

Berntsen, Lisa. 2016. "Reworking Labour Practices: On the Agency of Unorganized Mobile Migrant Construction Workers." *Work Employment & Society* 30 (3): 472–88.

Berntsen, Lisa, and Nathan Lillie. 2016. "Hyper-mobile Migrant Workers and Dutch Trade Union Representation Strategies at the Eemshaven Construction Sites." *Economic and Industrial Democracy* 37 (1): 171–87.

Bertossi, Christophe. 2010. "What If National Models of Integration Did Not Exist?" *Perspectives on Europe* 40 (2): 50–56.

Bieler, Andreas, Roland Erne, Darragh Golden, Idar Helle, Knut Kjeldstadli, Thiago Matos, and Sabina Stan. 2015. *Labor and Transnational Action in Times of Crisis.* London: Rowman and Littlefield.

Bigo, Didier. 2009. "Immigration Controls and Free Movement in Europe." *International Review of the Red Cross* 91 (875): 579–91.

Bigo, Didier. 2013. "Borders, Mobility and Security." In *A Political Sociology of Transnational Europe*, edited by Niilo Kauppi, 111–27. Essex, UK: ECPR Press.

Blanco, Victor S. 1997. "The Media Politics of Social Protest." *Mobilization: The International Journal of Theory and Research in Social Movements* 2 (2): 185–205.

Blume, Georg. 2013. "Ein Schlachthof macht dicht. In Frankreich sehen sich 900 entlassene Arbeiter als Opfer deutscher Niedriglöhner" [A slaughterhouse is closing. In France, 900 dismissed workers see themselves as victims of German low wage earners]. Zeit Online, November 2013. http://www.zeit.de/2013/45/niedriglohn-schlachthof-frankreich/komplettansicht.

Bogoeski, Vladimir. 2017. "Chain Liability as a Mechanism for Strengthening the Rights of Posted Workers: The German Chain Liability Model." PhD diss., Hertie School of Governance, Berlin. http://www.solidar.org/system/downloads/attachments/000/000/701/original/2017_09_26_PROMO_Briefing_Paper_Bogoeski_final.pdf?1506505471.

Bonacich, Edna. 1972. "A Theory of Ethnic Antagonism: The Split Labor Market." *American Sociological Review* 37 (5): 547–59.

Bosch, Gerhard, and Claudia Weinkopf, eds. 2008. *Low Wage Work in Germany*. New York: Russell Sage Foundation.

Bosch, Gerhard, Claudia Weinkopf, and Georg Worthmann. 2011. *Die Fragilität des Tarifsystems: Einhaltung von Entgeltstandards und Mindestlöhnen am Beispiel des Bauhauptgewerbes* [The fragility of the bargaining system: compliance with fee standards and minimum wages using the example of the main construction industry]. Berlin: Edition Sigma.

Bosch, Gerhard, and Robert Zühlke-Robinet. 2003. "Germany: The Labour Market in the German Construction Industry." In *Building Chaos: An International Comparison of Deregulation in the Construction Industry*, edited by Gerhard Bosch and Peter Philips, 48–72. London: Routledge.

Brehmer, Wolfram, and Herbert Seifert. 2007. "Wie prekär sind atypische Beschäftigungsverhältnisse? Eine empirische Analyse" [How precarious are atypical employment relationships? An empirical analysis]. WSI Working Paper 156 (November). Wirtschafts- und Sozial-wissenschaftliches Institut, Düsseldorf. https://www.boeckler.de/wsi_5126.htm?chunk=6&jahr=.

Brenner, Neil. 1999. "Globalisation as Reterritorialization: The Re-scaling of Urban Governance in the European Union." *Urban Studies* 36 (3): 431–51.

Brenner, Neil, Jamie Peck, and Nick Theodore. 2010. "Variegated Neoliberalisation: Geographies, Modalities, Pathways." *Global Networks* 10 (2): 182–222.

Brinkmann, Ulrich, and Oliver Nachtwey. 2013. "Post-democracy, Co-determination and Industrial Citizenship." *Politische Vierteljahresschrift* 54 (3): 506–33.

Brookes, Melissa. 2013. "Varieties of Power in Transnational Labour Alliances: An Analysis of Workers' Structural, Institutional, and Coalitional Power." *Global Economy Labour Studies Journal* 38 (3): 181–200.

Brümmer, Matthias. 2014. "Sozialdumping in der deutschen Fleischindustrie— Lohnsklaven machen deutsches Fleisch konkurrenzlos billig" [Social dumping in the German meat industry—Wage slaves make German meat unrivaled cheap]. In *Der kritische Agrarbericht 2014*, edited by Manuel Schneider, Andrea Fink-Keßler, Friedhelm Stodieck, 145–50. http://www.kritischer-agrarbericht.de/fileadmin/Daten-KAB/KAB-2014/KAB2014_145_150_Bruemmer.pdf.

Bryman, Alan. 2001. *Social Research Methods*. Oxford: Oxford University Press.

Bundesamt für Migration und Flüchtlinge. 2010. *Migrationsbericht 2010* [Migration report 2010]. Berlin: Bundesministerium des Innern.

Burgoon, Brian. 2013. "Inequality and Anti-globalization Backlash by Political Parties." *European Union Politics* 14 (3): 408–35.

Busemeyer, Markus R., and Christine Trampusch. 2013. "Liberalization by Exhaustion: Transformative Change in the German Welfare State and Vocational Training System." *Zeitschrift für Sozialreform* 59 (3): 291–312.

Butler, Judith. 1988. "Performative Acts and Gender Constitution: An Essay in Phenomenology and Feminist Theory." *Theatre Journal* 40 (4): 519–31."

Campbell, Jon L. 2009. "Institutional Reproduction and Change." In *The Oxford Handbook of Comparative Institutional Analysis*, edited by Glenn Morgan, John L. Campbell, Colin Crouch, Peer Hull Kristensen, Ove K. Pedersen, and Richard Whitley, 87–115. New York: Oxford University Press.

Caporaso, James A. 1996. "The European Union and Forms of State: Westphalian, Regulatory or Post-Modern?" *Journal of Common Market Studies* 34 (1): 29–52.

Çaro, Erka, Lisa Berntsen, Nathan Lillie, and Ines Wagner. 2015. "Posted Migration and Segregation in the European Construction Sector." *Journal of Ethnic and Migration Studies* 41 (10): 1600–20.

Cassarino, Jean-Pierre. 2006. "Approaching Borders and Frontiers: Notions and Implications." *Research Reports 2006/3 EUI RSCAS*. Florence: European University Institute.

Castles, Stephen. 2004. "Why Migration Policies Fail." *Ethnic and Racial Studies* 27 (2): 205–27.

Chemnitz, Christine, and Reinhild Benning, eds. 2014. *Fleischatlas: Daten und Fakten über Tiere als Nahrungsmittel* [Meat atlas: Figures and facts about animals as food]. Berlin: Le Monde Diplomatique/TAZ Verl.- und Vertriebs-GmbH.

Christiansen, Thomas, and Knut Jørgensen. 2000. "Transnational Governance 'Above' and 'Below' the State: The Changing Nature of Borders in the New Europe." *Regional and Federal Studies* 10 (2): 62–77.

Coe, Niel M., Peter Dicken, and Martin Hess. 2008. "Global Production Networks: Realizing the Potential." *Journal of Economic Geography* 8 (3): 271–95.

Coe, Niel M., Jennifer Johns, and Kevin Ward. 2012. "Limits to Expansion: Transnational Corporations and Territorial Embeddedness in the Japanese Temporary Staffing Market." *Global Networks* 12 (1): 22–47.

Cohen, Robin. 1987. *The New Helots: Migrants in the International Division Labour.* Aldershot, UK: Avebury.

Colling, Trevor, and Mike Terry, eds. 2010. *Industrial Relations: Theory and Practice.* Chichester: John Wiley & Sons.

Connolly, Heather, Stefania Marino, and Miguel Martinez Lucio. 2017. "'Justice for Janitors' Goes Dutch: The Possibilities and Limitations of an Organizing Approach in the Netherlands." *Work, Employment, Society* 31 (2): 319–35.

Cornelius, Wayne A. 1982. "Interviewing Undocumented Immigrants: Methodological Reflections Based on Fieldwork in Mexico and the U.S." *International Migration Review* 16 (2): 378–411.

Cott, Nancy F. 1998. "Marriage and Women's Citizenship in the United States, 1830–1934." *American Historical Review* 103 (5): 1473.

Cox, Kevin R., ed. 1997. *Spaces of Globalisation: Reasserting the Power of the Local.* New York: Guilford Press.

Cremers, Jan. 2009. Introduction to *The Free Movement of Workers in the European Union*, edited by Jan Cremers and Peter Donders, 7–15. Brussels: European Institute for Construction Labour Research: CLR Studies 4.

Cremers, Jan. 2011. *In Search of Cheap Labour in Europe: Working and Living Conditions of Posted Workers.* Brussels: CLR/EFBWW/International Books.

Cremers, Jan, Jon-Erik Dølvik, and Gerhard Bosch. 2007. "Posting of Workers in the Single Market: Attempts to Prevent Social Dumping and Regime Competition in the EU." *Industrial Relations Journal* 38 (6): 524–41.

Dälken, Michaela. 2012. *Grenzenlos faire Mobilität?* [Borderless fair mobility?] Berlin-Brandenburg: Deutscher Gewerkschaftsbund.

Danaj, Sonila, and Markku Sippola. 2015. "Organising Posted Workers in the Construction Sector." In *The Outsourcing Challenge: Organizing Workers across Fragmented Production Networks*, edited by Jan Drahokoupil, 217–335. Brussels: European Trade Union Institute.

Danaj, Sonila, and Ines Wagner. 2016. "Constructing the Underclass of 'Poverty Migrant': Discourses on Labour Migration and Welfare Policy in Germany and the UK." How Class Works 2016 Conference, Stony Brook, NY, June 8–11.

Datta, Kavita. 2009. "Risky Migrants? Low-Paid Migrant Workers Coping with Financial Exclusion in London." *European Urban and Regional Studies* 16 (4): 331–44.

Davies, Anne C. L. 2008. "One Step Forward, Two Steps Back? The *Viking* and *Laval* Cases in the ECJ." *Industrial Law Journal* 37 (2): 126–48.

DeCerteau, Michel. 1984. *The Practice of Everyday Life*. Berkeley: University of California Press.

Deeg, Richard, and Gregory Jackson. 2007. "Toward a More Dynamic Theory of Capitalist Variety." *Socio-Economic Review* 5 (1): 149–79.

Del Sarto, Raffaella A. 2013. "Defining Borders and People in the Borderlands: EU Policies, Israeli Prerogatives and the Palestinians." *Journal of Common Market Studies* 52 (2): 200–216.

Deutscher Bundestag. 2013. *Mindestlöhne durchsetzen, Qualität der Kontrollen verbessern* [Enforce minimum wages, improve quality of controls]. Kleine Anfrage der Abgeordneten Beate Müller-Gemmeke, Dr. Wolfgang Strengmann-Kuhn, Brigitte Pothmer, weiterer Abgeordneter und der Fraktion BÜNDNIS 90/DIE GRÜNEN [Enforce minimum wage. Improve the quality of controls. Governmental question by Member of Parliament Beate Müller-Gemmeke, dr. Wolfgang Strengmann-Kuhn, Brigitte Pothmer, another member of parliament and of BÜNDNIS 90/DIE GRÜNEN]. Drucksache 17/12834.

Deutscher Gewerkschaftsbund (German Federation of Trade Unions). 2016. "DGB-Mitgliederzahlen 1994–2015" [DGB membership numbers 1994–2015]. http://www.dgb.de/uber-uns/dgb-heute/mitgliederzahlen/2010.

Diani, Mario. 1990. "The Italian Ecology Movement: From Radicalism to Moderation." In *Green Politics One*, edited by W. Rüdig, 153–76. Carbondale: Southern Illinois University Press.

Directive 96/71/EC of December 16, 1996, concerning the posting of workers in the framework of the provision of services. https://eur-lex.europa.eu/legal-content/en/ALL/?uri=CELEX%3A31996L0071.

Directive 2014/67/EU of May 15, 2014, on the enforcement of Directive 96/71/EC concerning the posting of workers in the framework of the provision of services. http://eur-lex.europa.eu/legal-content/EN/TXT/?uri=celex%3A32014L0066.

Djelic, Marie L., and Sigrid Quack. 2002. "The Missing Link: Bringing Institutions Back into the Debate on Economic Globalisation." Discussion Paper FS I 02–107. Berlin: Wissenschaftszentrum Berlin für Sozialforschung.

Doelfs, Guntram. 2012. "Werkverträge. 1,02 Euro pro Schwein" [Subcontracts. 1.02 Euro per pig]. *Magazin Mitbestimmung*, no. 12. http://www.boeckler.de/41784_41843 .htm.

Doelfs, Guntram. 2014. "Werkvertragsnehmer mit im Boot" [Subcontractor with on board. Magazine co-determination]. *Magazin Mitbestimmung*, no. 4. http://www .boeckler.de/46892_46911.htm.

Doellgast, Virginia. 2009. *Disintegrating Democracy at Work: Labour Unions and the Future of Good Jobs in the Service Economy.* Ithaca, NY: ILR Press/Cornell University Press.

Doellgast, Virginia, and Ian Greer. 2007. "Vertical Disintegration and the Disorganization of German Industrial Relations." *British Journal of Industrial Relations* 45 (1): 55–76.

Doeringer, Peter, and Michael J. Piore. 1971. *Internal Labour Markets and Manpower Analysis.* Boston: Heath Lexington Books.

Dølvik, Jon-Erik, and Line Eldring. 2006. "Industrial Relations Responses to Migration and Posting of Workers after EU Enlargement: Nordic Trends and Differences." *Transfer: European Review of Labour and Research* 12 (2): 213–30.

Dølvik, Jon-Erik, and Jelle Visser. 2009. "Free Movement, Equal Treatment and Workers' Rights: Can the European Union Solve Its Trilemma of Fundamental Principles?" *Industrial Relations Journal* 40 (6): 491–509.

Donders, Peter, and Karin Sengers. 2009. "Research on Implementation of Posting Directive 96/71/EC." In *The Free Movement of Workers in the European Union*, edited by Jan Cremers and Peter Donders, 15–56. Brussels: European Institute for Construction Labour Research: CLR Studies 4.

Dörre, Klaus. 2005a. "Prekariat—Eine arbeitspolitische Herausforderung" [Precariat— A labor political challenge]. *WSI Mitteilungen* 5: 250–58.

Dörre, Klaus. 2005b. "Entsicherte Arbeitsgesellschaft. Politik der Entprekarisierung" [Unsecured work society. Politics of de-precarisation]. *Widerspruch* 49: 5–18.

Dubois, Vincent. 2010. *The Bureaucrat and the Poor: Encounters in French Welfare Offices.* Farnham and Burlington, VT: Ashgate.

EFFAT (European Federation of Food, Agriculture, and Tourism). 2013. "Belgian Ministers' Condemnation of Germany's Social Dumping Practices Is Reminder to Act." Press release, March 26. http://www.effat.org/sites/default/files/news/9933/press -release-belgian-ministers-denounce-social-dumping-en.pdf.

Eichhorst, Werner. 2000. *Europäische Sozialpolitik zwischen nationaler Autonomie und Marktfreiheit: Die Entsendung von Arbeitnehmern in der EU* [European social policy between national autonomy and market freedom: The posting of workers in the EU]. Cologne: Campus.

Eichhorst, Werner. 2005. "Gleicher Lohn für gleiche Arbeit am gleichen Ort? Die Entsendung von Arbeitnehmern in der Europäischen Union." *Zeitschrift für Arbeitsmarktforschung* 33 (2/3): 197–217.

Eichhorst, Werner, and L. C. Kaiser. 2006. "The German Labour Market: Still Adjusting Badly?" Institute for Labor Economics Discussion Paper No. 2215, Bonn, Germany.

Eisenhardt, Kathleen M. 1989. "Building Theories from Case Study Research." *Academy of Management Review* 14 (4): 532–50.

Elden, Stuart. 2005. "Missing the Point: Globalization, Deterritorialization and the Space of the World." *Transactions of the Institute of British Geographers* 30 (1): 8–19.

Eldring, Line, Ian Fitzgerald, Jens Arnholtz, and Nana Hansen. 2012. "Post-accession Migration in Construction and Trade Union Responses in Denmark, Norway and the UK." *European Journal of Industrial Relations* 18 (1): 21–36.

Ellermann, Antje. 2015. "Do Policy Legacies Matter? Past and Present Guest Worker Recruitment in Germany." *Journal of Ethnic and Migration Studies* 41 (8): 1235–53.

Emmenegger, Patrick, Silje Häusermann, Bruno Palier, and Martin Seeleib-Kaiser. 2012. "How We Grow Unequal." In *The Age of Dualisation: The Changing Face of Inequality in Deindustrializing Societies*, edited by Patrick Emmenegger, Silje Häusermann, Bruno Palier, and Martin Seeleib-Kaiser, 3–27. Oxford: Oxford University Press.

Engels, Dietrich, Regine Köller, Ruud Koopmans, and Jutta Höhne. 2012. *Zweiter Integrationsindikatorenbericht, erstellt für die Beauftragte der Bundesregierung für Migration, Flüchtlinge und Integration* [Second Integration Indicator Report, prepared for the Federal Government Commissioner for Migration, Refugees and Integration]. Paderborn, Germany: Bonifatius GmbH.

Erne, Roland. 2008. *European Unions, Labor's Quest for a Transnational Democracy.* Ithaca, NY: ILR Press/Cornell University Press.

European Commission. 2012. *Posting of Workers in the European Union and EFTA Countries: Report on A1 Portable Documents Issued in 2010 and 2011.* Brussels: European Commission.

European Parliament. 2013a. "Complaint of Social Dumping Filed against Germany by Belgian Ministers." Parliamentary Questions E-004208-13, December 4, 2013. http://www.europarl.europa.eu/sides/getDoc.do?pubRef=-//EP//TEXT+WQ+E-2013-004208+0+DOC+XML+V0//EN.

European Parliament. 2013b. "Motion for a European Parliament Resolution on Effective Labour Inspection as a Strategy to Improve Workers' Rights (2013/2112(INI))." http://www.europarl.europa.eu/sides/getDoc.do?pubRef=//EP//NONSGML+COMPARL+PE-516.942+01+DOC+PDF+V0//EN.

Expert Council on Integration and Migration. 2013. *Erfolgsfall Europa? Folgen und Herausforderungen der EU-Freizügigkeit für Deutschland* [Successful Europe? Consequences and challenges of EU free movement for Germany]. Annual Report. https://www.svr-migration.de/wp-content/uploads/2017/05/SVR_Jahresgutachten_2013.pdf.

Faist, Thomas. 2008. "Dual Citizenship in an Age of Mobility." In *Delivering Citizenship: The Transatlantic Council on Migration*, edited by Bertelsmann Stiftung, European Policy Centre and Migration Policy Institute, 73–98. Gütersloh, Germany: Verlag Bertelsmann Stiftung.

Favell, Adrian. 2008. *Eurostars and Eurocities: Free Movement and Mobility in an Integrating Europe.* Oxford: Oxford University Press.

Favell, Adrian, and Randall Hansen. 2002. "Markets against Politics: Migration, EU Enlargement and the Idea of Europe." *Journal of Ethnic and Migration Studies* 29 (4): 581–602.

Federal Statistical Office [Statistisches Bundesamt]. 2014. "Fachserie 1, Reihe 2: Bevölkerung und Erwerbstätigkeit 2013. Ausländische Bevölkerung. Ergebnisse des

Ausländerzentralregisters" [Subject series 1, No. 2: Population and Employment 2013. Foreign population. Results of the Central Register of Foreigners]. https://www .destatis.de/GPStatistik/receive/DEHeft_heft_00022963.

Federal Statistical Office [Statistisches Bundesamt]. 2016a. "Bauhauptgewerbe / Ausbaugewerbe / Bauträger. Lange Reihen der jährlichen Betriebserhebungen 2016" [Construction / Finishing / Property Developers. Long rows of annual business surveys 2016]. https://www.destatis.de/DE/Publikationen/Thematisch/Bauen/Baugewerbe Struktur/LangeReihenBetriebserhebungBauAusbaugewerbe.html.

Federal Statistical Office [Statistisches Bundesamt]. 2016b. "Produzierendes Gewerbe. Tätige Personen und Umsatz der Betriebe im Baugewerbe 2015. Fachserie 4, Reihe 5.1" [Manufacturing: Employees and turnover of companies in the construction industry in 2015. Subject series 4, No. 5.1]. https://www.destatis.de/DE/Publikationen/Thematisch /Bauen/BaugewerbeStruktur/PersonenUmsatzBaugewerbe2040510167004.pdf?__blob =publicationFile.

Fellini, Ivana, Anna Ferro, and Giovanna Fullin. 2007. "Recruitment Processes and Labour Mobility: The Construction Industry in Europe." *Work, Employment and Society* 21 (2): 277–98.

Fine, Janice. 2006. *Worker Centers: Organizing Communities at the Edge of the Dream.* Ithaca, NY: ILR Press/Cornell University Press.

Fiss, Peer, and Edward J. Zajak. 2004. "The Diffusion of Ideas over Contested Terrain: The (Non)Adoption of a Shareholder Value Orientation among German Firms." *Administrative Science Quarterly* 49 (4): 501–34.

Fitzgerald, Ian, and Jane Hardy. 2010. "Thinking Outside the Box? Trade Union Organizing Strategies and Polish Migrant Workers in the United Kingdom." *British Journal of Industrial Relations* 48 (1): 131–50.

Flecker, Jörg, and Pamela Meil. 2010. "Organisational Restructuring and Emerging Service Value Chains: Implications for Work and Employment." *Work Employment and Society* 24 (4): 680–98.

Freeman, Gary P. 1995. "Modes of Immigration Politics in Liberal Democratic States." *International Migration Review* 29 (4): 881–913.

Frege, Carola, Heery Edmund, and Lowell Turner. 2004. "Coalition Building in Comparative Perspective." In *Varieties of Unionism: Strategies for Labour Movement Renewal in the Global North*, edited by C. Frege and J. Kelly, 137–58. New York: Oxford University Press.

Frege, Carola, and J. Kelly. 2003. "Union Revitalization Strategies in Comparative Perspective." *European Journal of Industrial Relations* 9 (1): 7–24.

Fuller, Gillian. 2003. "Life in Transit: Between Airport and Camp." *Borderlands E-journal* 2 (1).

Galgóczi, Béla, Janine Leschke, and Andrew Watt. 2009. *EU Labour Migration since Enlargement: Trends, Impacts and Policies.* Aldershot, UK: Ashgate.

Gautié, Jérome, and John Schmitt. 2010. *Low-Wage Work in the Wealthy World.* New York: Russell Sage Foundation.

Geddes, Andrew. 2005. "Europe's Border Relationships and International Migration Relations." *Journal of Common Market Studies* 43 (4): 787–806.

Gereffi, Gary, John Humphrey, and Timothy Sturgeon. 2005. "The Governance of Global Value Chains." *Review of International Political Economy* 12 (1): 78–104.

Gleadle, Kathryn. 2009. *Borderline Citizen: Women, Gender and Political Culture in Britain, 1815–1867*. Oxford and New York: Oxford University Press.

Glick, William H., George P. Huber, Chet C. Miller, Harold D. Doty, and Kathleen M. Sutcliffe. 1990. "Studying Changes in Organizational Design and Effectiveness: Retrospective Event Histories and Periodic Assessments." *Organization Science* 1 (3): 293–312.

Glick Schiller, Nina, N. Basch, and Szanton Blanc. 1995. "From Immigrant to Transmigrant: Theorizing Transnational Migration." *Anthropological Quarterly* 68 (1): 48–63.

Goldstein, Kenneth. 2002. "Getting in the Door: Sampling and Completing Elite Interviews." *Political Science and Politics* 35 (4): 669–72.

Greer, Ian. 2008. "Social Movement Unionism and Social Partnership in Germany: The Case of Hamburg's Hospitals." *Industrial Relations* 47 (4): 602–24.

Greer, Ian, Zinovius Ciupijus, and Nathan Lillie. 2013. "The European Migrant Workers Union: Union Organizing through Labour Transnationalism." *European Journal of Industrial Relations* 19 (1): 5–20.

Greif, Avner, and David Laitin. 2004. "A Theory of Endogenous Institutional Change." *American Political Science Review* 98 (4): 633–52.

Greven, Ludwig. 2014. "Sie wollen nur überleben auf dem Arbeitsstrich in Hamburg: Hier suchen Rumänen und Bulgaren nach Arbeit. Die deutsche Wirtschaft beutet sie aus. Hartz IV bekommt niemand" [They only want to survive on the labor strip in Hamburg: Here, Romanians and Bulgarians are looking for work. The German economy exploits them. Nobody gets Hartz IV]. Zeit Online, January 17, 2014. http://www.zeit.de/politik/deutschland/2014–01/mirgranten-osteuropa-wilhelmsburg.

Grimshaw, David, and Jill Rubery. 2005. "Intercapital Relations and the Network Organisation: Re-defining the Work and Employment Nexus." *Cambridge Journal of Economics* 29 (6): 1027–90.

Grunert, Klaus, Susan James, and Philip Moss. 2010. "Tough Meat, Hard Candy: Implications for Low-Wage Work in the Food-Processing Industry." In *Low-Wage Work in the Wealthy World*, edited by Jérome Gautié and John Schmitt, 367–420. New York: Russell Sage Foundation.

Guild, Elspeth. 2001. "Moving the Borders of Europe." Inaugural lecture held at the University of Nijmegen, Nijmegen, the Netherlands, May 30.

Guild, Elspeth. 2009. *Security and Migration in the 21st Century*. Cambridge, MA: Polity.

Gumbrell-McCormick, Rebecca. 2011. "European Trade Unions and 'Atypical' Workers." *Industrial Relations Journal* 42 (3): 293–310.

Gumbrell-McCormick, Rebecca, and Richard Hyman. 2013. *Trade Unions in Western Europe*. Oxford: Oxford University Press.

Güster, Claus-Harald. 2015. "Tarifpolitik im Jahr 1 des Mindestlohn" [Collective bargaining policy in year 1 of the minimum wage]. WSI Tarifpolitische Tagung 2015 [WSI Collective Bargaining Conference 2015]. Düsseldorf: Institute of Economic and Social Research.

Hacker, Jacob S. 2005. "Policy Drift: The Hidden Politics of US Welfare State Retrenchment." In *Beyond Continuity: Institutional Change in Advanced Political Economies*, edited by Wolfgang Streeck and Kathleen Thelen, 40–83. Oxford: Oxford University Press.

Hall, Peter, and David Soskice. 2001. *Varieties of Capitalism: The Institutional Foundations of Comparative Advantage.* Oxford: Oxford University Press.

Hamann, Karen. 2010. "The European Red Meat Industry. Present Situation and Factors Shaping the Industry, August 2010." EFFAT Charter against Precarious Work, adopted by the 3rd EFFAT Congress, 20–21.10.2009. In author's possession.

Hanau, Peter. 1997. "Sozialdumping im Binnenmarkt" [Social dumping in the single market]. In *Recht und Wirtschaft der Europäischen Union*, edited by J. F. Baur and C. Watrin, 145–68. Berlin: R. I. Z. Schriften, Bd. 6.

Hardy, Jane, Line Eldring, and Thorsten Schulten. 2012. "Trade Union Responses to Migrant Workers from the 'New Europe': A Three Sector Comparison in Norway, Germany and the UK." *European Journal of Industrial Relations* 18 (4): 347–63.

Harvey, David. 1982. *The Limits to Capital.* Oxford: Basil Blackwell.

Hassel, Anke. 2014. "The Paradox of Liberalization: Understanding Dualism and the Recovery of the German Political Economy." *British Journal of Industrial Relations* 52 (1): 57–81.

Hassel, Anke, Jette Steen Knudsen, and Bettina Wagner. 2016. "Winning the Battle or Losing the War: The Impact of European Integration on Labour Market Institutions in Germany and Denmark." *Journal of European Public Policy* 23 (8): 1218–39.

Hauptverband der deutschen Bauindustrie. 2015. *Tarifsammlung für die Bauwirtschaft 2014/2015* [Collective rate for the construction industry, 2014/2015]. Berlin: Elsner.

Held, David. 1992. "Democracy: From City-States to a Cosmopolitan Order?" *Political Studies* 40 (1): 10–39.

Herod, Andrew. 1998. "The Spatiality of Labor Unionism." In *Organizing the Landscape: Geographical Perspectives on Labor Unionism*, edited by Andrew Herod, 1–36. Minneapolis: University of Minnesota.

Hetherington, Kevin. 2003. *The Badlands of Modernity: Heterotopia and Social Ordering.* London: Routledge.

Hirschman, Albert O. 1970. *Exit, Voice, and Loyalty. Responses to Decline in Firms, Organizations, and States.* Cambridge, MA: Harvard University Press.

Hoffmann, Jürgen. 2006. "The Relevance of the Exit Option: The Challenges for European Trade Unions of Post-Fordist, Internationalisation of the Economy and Financial Market Capitalism." *Transfer: European Review of Labour and Research* 12 (4): 609–20.

Holgate, Jane. 2005. "Organising Migrant Workers: A Case Study of Working Conditions and Unionisation at a Sandwich Factory in London." *Work, Employment & Society* 19 (3): 463–80.

Holst, Hajo. 2014. "Commodifying Institutions: Vertical Disintegration and Institutional Change in German Labour Relations." *Work, Employment and Society* 28 (1): 13–20.

Höpner, Martin, and Armin Schäfer. 2007. "A New Phase of European Integration: Organized Capitalisms in Post-Ricardian Europe." MPIfG Discussion Paper 07/4, MPIfG (Max Planck Institute for the Study of Societies), Cologne.

Höpner, Martin, and Armin Schäfer. 2008. *Die politische Ökonomie der europäischen Integration.* Frankfurt/New York: Campus.

Höpner, Martin, and Armin Schäfer. 2012. "Embeddedness in Regional Integration: Waiting for Polayni in a Hayekian Setting." *International Organisation* 66 (3): 429–55.

Houwerzijl, Mijke, Saskia Peters, and Yves Jorens. 2012. *Study on the Protection of Workers' Rights in Subcontracting Processes in the European Union.* Brussels: European Commission.

Huws, Ursula, Jörg Flecker, and Simone Dahlmann. 2004. *Status Report on Outsourcing of ICT and Related Services in the EU.* Dublin: European Foundation for the Improvement of Living and Working Conditions.

Huysmans, Jef. 2006. *The Politics of Insecurity.* London: Routledge.

IDEA Consult and ECORYS Netherlands. 2011. *Study on the Economic and Social Effects Associated with the Phenomenon of Posting of Workers in the EU.* Study to the European Commission Contract Number VT/2009/062, 2011.

Isin, Engin. 2009. "Citizenship in Flux: The Figure of the Activist Citizen." *Subjectivity* 29: 367–88.

Ismeri Europa. 2012. *Preparatory Study for an Impact Assessment Concerning the Possible Revision of the Legislative Framework on the Posting of Workers in the Context of the Provision of Services.* Report on behalf of the European Commission.

Jackson, Gregory. 2005. "Contested Boundaries: Ambiguity and Creativity in the Evolution of German Codetermination." In *Beyond Continuity: Institutional Change in Advanced Political Economies,* edited by W. Streeck and K. Thelen, 229–55. Oxford: Oxford University Press.

Jackson, Gregory. 2010. "Actors and Institutions." In *The Oxford Handbook of Comparative Institutional Analysis,* edited by G. Morgan, J. Campbell, C. Crouch, O. K. Pedersen, and R. Whitley, 63–87. Oxford: Oxford University Press.

Jackson, Gregory, Sarosh Kuruvilla, and Carola Frege. 2013. "Across Boundaries: The Global Challenges Facing Workers and Employment Research." *British Journal of Industrial Relations* 51 (3): 425–39. doi:10.1111/bjir.12039.

Jaehrling, Karen, and Patrick Méhaut. 2012. "Varieties of Institutional Avoidance: Employers' Strategies in Low-Waged Service Sector Occupations in France and Germany." *Socio-Economic Review* 11 (4): 1–24.

Jaehrling, Karen, Claudia Weinkopf, Ines Wagner, Gerhard Bosch, and Thorsten Kalina. 2016. *Reducing Precarious Work in Europe through Social Dialogue: The Case of Germany.* Report for the European Commission, Institute of Work, Skills and Training, University of Duisburg-Essen.

Jenkins, Jane. 2013. "Organizing Spaces of Hope: Union Formation by Indian Garment Workers." *British Journal of Industrial Relations* 51 (3): 623–43.

Joerges, Christian, and Florian Rödl. 2009. "Informal Politics, Formalised Law and the 'Social Deficit' of European Integration: Reflections after the Judgments of the ECJ in Viking and Laval." *European Law Journal* 15 (1): 1–19.

Johnston, Paul. 2002. "Citizenship Movement Unionism: For the Defense of Local Communities in the Global Age." In *Unions in a Globalized Environment: Changing Borders, Organizational Boundaries and Social Roles,* edited by B. Nissen, 236–63. Armonk, NY: M. E. Sharpe.

Kahanec, Martin. 2013. "Labour Mobility in an Enlarged European Union." In *International Handbook on the Economics of Migration,* edited by A. Constant and K. Zimmermann, 137–52. Cheltenham: Edward Elgar.

Kahanec, Martin, Anzelike Zaiceva, and Klaus F. Zimmermann. 2010. "Lessons from Migration after EU Enlargement." In *EU Labour Markets after Post-Enlargement Migration*, edited by Martin Kahanec and Klaus F. Zimmermann, 3–46. London: Springer.

Kahanec, Martin, and Klaus F. Zimmermann. 2009. *Migration in an Enlarged EU: A Challenging Solution?* Economic Papers 363. Brussels: European Commission, Directorate-General for Economic and Financial Affairs.

Kahmann, Markus. 2006. "The Posting of Workers in the German Construction Industry." *Transfer: European Review of Labour and Research* 12 (2): 183–96.

Kall, Kairit, and Nathan Lillie. 2017. "Protection of Posted Workers in the European Union: Findings and Policy Recommendations Based on Existing Research." PROMO briefing paper. Accessed February 28, 2018. http://www.solidar.org/system /downloads/attachments/000/000/700/original/2017_09_26_PROMO_Briefing _Paper__Kall_final.pdf?1506505471.

Kalleberg, Arne. 2001. "Organizing Flexibility: The Flexible Firm in a New Century." *British Journal of Industrial Relations* 39 (4): 479–504.

Katz, Cindi. 2004. *Growing Up Global: Economic Restructuring and Children's Everyday Lives*. Minneapolis: University of Minnesota Press.

Katz, Harry, Thomas Kochan, and Alexander Colvin. 2008. *An Introduction to Collective Bargaining and Industrial Relations*. New York: McGraw Hill.

Katzenstein, Peter J. 1987. *Policy and Politics in West Germany: The Growth of a Semisovereign State*. Philadelphia: Temple University Press.

Kauppi, Niilo. 2010. "The Political Ontology of European Integration." *Comparative European Politics* 8 (1): 19–36.

Kauppi, Niilo. 2013. Introduction to *A Political Sociology of Transnational Europe*, edited by N. Kauppi, 3–17. Essex: ECPR Press.

Keune, Maarten. 2015. "Trade Unions, Precarious Work and Dualisation in Europe." In *Non-standard Employment in Post-Industrial Labour Markets: An Occupational-Perspective*, edited by W. Eichhorst and P. Marx, 378–401. Northampton, MA: Edward Elgar.

Kilpatrick, Claire. 2009. "Laval's Regulatory Conundrum: Collective Standard-Setting and the Court's New Approach to Posted Workers." *European Law Review* 34 (6): 844–65.

King, Desmond, and David Rueda. 2008. "Cheap Labour: The New Politics of 'Bread and Roses' in Industrial Democracies." *Perspectives on Politics* 6 (2): 279–97.

Kitschelt, Herbert, and Wolfgang Streeck. 2003. "From Stability to Stagnation: Germany at the Beginning of the Twenty-First Century." *West European Politics* 26 (4): 1–34.

Kohler-Koch, Beate. 2005. "European Governance and System Integration." *European Governance Papers*, no. C-05–01. http://www.connex-network.org/eurogov/pdf/egp -connex-C-05-01.pdf.

Korpi, Walter. 1998. "Power Resources Approach vs. Action and Conflict: On Causal and Intentional Explanations in the Study of Power." In *Power Resource Theory and the Welfare State: A Critical Approach*, edited by J. S. O'Connor and G. M. Olsen, 37–65. Toronto: University of Toronto Press.

Korpi, Walter. 2006. "Power Resources and Employer-Centered Approaches in Explanations of Welfare States and Varieties of Capitalism: Protagonists, Consenters, and Antagonists." *World Politics* 58 (2): 167–206.

Kostadinova, Valentina. 2013. "The European Commission and the Configuration of Internal European Union Borders: Direct and Indirect Contribution." *Journal of Common Market Studies* 51: 264–80.

Krings, Torben. 2009. "A Race to the Bottom? Trade Unions, EU Enlargement and the Free Movement of Labour." *European Journal of Industrial Relations* 15 (1): 49–69.

Krings, Torben. 2013. "East-West Mobility and the (Re-)regulation of Employment in Transnational Labour Markets." *Comparative Social Research* 32: 183–213.

Lannes, Xavier. 1956. "International Mobility of Manpower in Western Europe: II." *International Labour Review* 73 (2): 135–51.

Lee, Aadler H., Maite Tapia, and Lowell Turner. 2014. *Mobilizing against Inequality: Unions, Immigrant Workers, and the Crisis of Capitalism*. Ithaca, NY: Cornell University Press.

Lefebvre, Bruno. 2006. "Posted Workers in France." *Transfer: European Review of Labour and Research* 12 (2): 197–212.

Le Queux, Stephanie, and Ivan Sainsaulieu. 2010. "Social Movement and Unionism in France: A Case for Revitalization?" *Labour Studies Journal* 35 (4): 503–19.

Lier, David C. 2007. "Places of Work, Scales of Organising: A Review of Labour Geography." *Geography Compass* 1 (4): 814–33.

Lillie, Nathan. 2010. "Bringing the Offshore Ashore: Transnational Production, Industrial Relations and the Reconfiguration of Sovereignty." *International Studies Quarterly* 54 (3): 683–704.

Lillie, Nathan. 2011. "European Integration and Transnational Labour Markets." In *Transnational Europe: Promise, Paradox, Limits*, edited by A. Hurrelmann and J. DeBardeleben, 113–31. Basingstoke, Hampshire: Palgrave Macmillan.

Lillie, Nathan, and Ian Greer. 2007. "Industrial Relations, Migration, and Neoliberal Politics: The Case of the European Construction Sector." *Politics & Society* 35 (4): 551–81.

Lillie, Nathan, Ines Wagner, and Lisa Berntsen. 2014. "The Logic of Inappropriateness: Migration and the Politics of Labour Relations in the European Construction Industry." In *The Comparative Political Economy of Work and Employment Relations*, edited by M. Hauptmaier and M. Vidal, 312–32. Basingstoke, UK: Palgrave Macmillan.

Lindemann, Kai. 2013. "Migration, Solidarität und Gewerkschaften" [Migration, solidarity, and trade unions]. Heinrich Böll Stiftung, Migrationspolitisches Portal, September 10. https://heimatkunde.boell.de/2013/09/10/migration-solidaritaet-und -gewerkschaften.

Lipsky, Michael. 1980. *Street-Level Bureaucracy: Dilemmas of the Individual in Public Services*. New York: Russell Sage Foundation.

Mack, Natascha, Cynthia Woodsong, Kathleen MacQueen, Greg Guest, and Emily Namey. 2005. *Qualitative Research Methods: A Data Collector's Field Guide*. Research Triangle Park, NC: USAID, Family Health International.

MacKenzie, R. 2010. "Why Do Contingent Workers Join a Trade Union? Evidence from the Irish Telecommunications Sector?" *European Journal of Industrial Relations* 16 (2): 153–68.

Marchington, Mick, Damian Grimshaw, Jill Rubery, and Hugh Willmott, eds. 2005. *Fragmenting Work: Blurring Organizational Boundaries and Disordering Hierarchies.* Oxford: Oxford University Press.

Marginson, Paul, and Keith Sisson. 2004. *European Integration and Industrial Relations: Multi-level Governance in the Making.* Basingstoke, Hampshire: Palgrave Macmillan.

Marino, Stefania. 2015. "Trade Unions, Special Structures and the Inclusion of Migrant Workers: On the Role of Union Democracy." *Work, Employment & Society* 29 (5): 826–42.

Marino, Stefania, Judith Roosblad, and Rinus Penninx, eds. 2017. *Trade Unions and Migrant Workers: New Contexts and Challenges in Europe.* Cheltenham, UK: Edward Elgar.

Martinez Lucio, M., and Robert Mackenzie. 2004. "Unstable Boundaries? Evaluating the 'New Regulation' within Employment Relations." *Economy and Society* 33 (1): 77–97.

Massey, Doreen. 1994. *Space, Place and Gender.* Cambridge, MA: Polity Press.

McCammon, Holly J., and Karen E. Campbell. 2002. "Allies on the Road to Victory: Coalition Formation between the Suffragists and the Woman's Christian Temperance Union." *Mobilization* 7 (3): 231–51.

McGovern, Patrick. 2007. "Immigration, Labour Markets and Employment Relations: Problems and Prospects." *British Journal of Industrial Relations* 45 (2): 217–35.

McGrath-Champ, Susan, Andrew Herod, and Al Rainnie. 2010. *Handbook of Employment and Society: Working Space.* Cheltenham, UK: Edward Elgar.

Meardi, Guglielmo. 2012. "Union Immobility? Trade Unions and the Freedoms of Movement in the Enlarged EU." *British Journal of Industrial Relations* 50 (1): 99–120.

Meardi, Guglielmo, Antonio Martin, and Mariona Lozano Riera. 2012. "Constructing Uncertainty: Unions and Migrant Labour in Construction in Spain and the UK." *Journal of Industrial Relations* 54 (5): 5–21.

Menz, Georg. 2001. "Beyond the *Anwerbestopp*? The German-Polish Labor Treaty." *Journal of European Social Policy* 11 (3): 253–69.

Menz, Georg. 2005. *Varieties of Capitalism and Europeanization.* Oxford: Oxford University Press.

Menz, Georg. 2010. "After Agenda 2010 Is before the Elections: Consolidation, Dissent, and the Politics of German Labour Market Policy under the Grand Coalition." *German Politics* 19 (3–4): 446–59.

Merriam, Sharan B. 1988. *Case Study Research in Education: A Qualitative Approach.* San Francisco: Jossey-Bass.

Miles, Matthew B., and Andrew M. Huberman. 1994. *Qualitative Data Analysis.* 2nd ed. London: Sage.

Milkman, Ruth. 2006. *L.A. Story: Immigrant Workers and the Future of the U.S. Labor Movement.* New York: Russell Sage Foundation.

Mills, Colleen. 2002. "The Hidden Dimension of Blue-Collar Sensemaking about Workplace Communication." *Journal of Business Communication* 39 (3): 288–313.

Minghi, Julian V. 1963. "Boundary Studies in Political Geography." *Annals of Association of American Geographers* 54: 407–28.

Mrozowicki, Adam, and Geert van Hootegem. 2008. "Unionism and Workers' Strategies in Capitalist Transformation: The Polish Case Reconsidered." *European Journal of Industrial Relations* 14 (2): 197–216.

Mundlak, Guy. 2009. "De-territorializing Labour Law." *Law & Ethics of Human Rights* 3 (2): Artikel 4.

Murray, Craig D., and Joanne Wynne. 2001. "Using an Interpreter to Research Community, Work and Family." *Community, Work and Family* 4 (2): 157–70.

Mussche, Ninke, Vincent Corluy, and Ive Marx. 2017. "How Posting Shapes a Hybrid Single European Labour Market." *European Journal of Industrial Relations*, May 24. https://doi.org/10.1177/0959680117708374.

Nadalutti, Elisabetta. 2013. "The European Grouping of Territorial Cooperation: Does the Nation State Still Count?" *Journal of Common Market Studies* 51 (4): 756–71.

NGG (Gewerkschaft Nahrung-Genuss-Gaststätten). 2012. "Einsatz von Werkverträgen in der Ernährungsindustrie" [Use of work subcontracts in the food industry]. Press release, Hamburg. http://www.ngg-bremen.de/w/files/region_bremen/werkvertraege_kurz_fin.pdf.

NGG (Gewerkschaft Nahrung-Genuss-Gaststätten). 2013. *Wenig Rechte Wenig Lohn: Wie Unternehmen Werkverträge (aus)nutzen* [Little rights, little pay: How companies exploit subcontracts]. Hamburg: Druckerei Sleppmann GmbH.

NGG (Gewerkschaft Nahrung-Genuss-Gaststätten). 2014. "Güster: Arbeitgeber sind in der Pflicht. Branchenmindestlohn Fleisch verzögert sich" [Güster: Employers are in the duty. Minimum wage meat is delayed]. Press release, June 26. https://www.ngg.net/pressemitteilungen/2014/2quartal/26-6-chg/.

Oliver, Christine. 1991. "Strategic Responses to Institutional Processes." *Academy of Management Review* 16 (1): 145–79.

Ong, Aihwa. 2006. *Neoliberalism as Exception: Mutations in Citizenship and Sovereignty*. Durham, NC: Duke University Press.

Ó Tuathail, Gearoid. 1998. "Political Geography III: Dealing with Deterritorialization." *Progress in Human Geography* 22 (1): 81–93.

Paasi, Aanssi. 1996. *Territories, Boundaries and Consciousness: The Changing Geographies of the Finnish-Russian Border*. New York: Wiley.

Pacolet, Jozef, and Frederic De Wispelaere. 2016. "Posting of Workers." *Report on A1 Portable Documents Issued in 2015*. Brussels: European Commission.

Palan, Ronan. 2003. *The Offshore World: Sovereign Markets, Virtual Places and Nomad Millionaires*. Ithaca, NY: Cornell University Press.

Palier, Bruno, and Kathleen Thelen. 2010. "Institutionalizing Dualism: Complementarities and Change in France and Germany." *Politics & Society* 38 (1): 119–48.

Pasquier, Romain, and Julien Weisbein. 2004. "L'Europe au microscope du local. Manifeste pour une sociologie politique de l'intégration communautaire" [Europe under the microscope of the local. Manifesto for a political sociology of community integration]. *Politique européenne* 1 (12): 5–12.

Pedersini, Roberto. 2010. *Posted Workers in the European Union*. Dublin: Eurofound.

Phillips, Deborah. 2010. "Minority Ethnic Segregation, Integration and Citizenship: A European Perspective." *Journal of Ethnic and Migration Studies* 36 (2): 209–25.

Pierson, Paul. 2004. *Politics in Time: History, Institutions, and Social Analysis*. Princeton, NJ: Princeton University Press.

Pile, Steve, and Michael Keith, eds. 1997. *Geographies of Resistance*. London: Routledge.

Piore, Michael. 1979. *Birds of Passage: Migrant Labour and Industrial Societies.* Cambridge: Cambridge University Press.

Pries, Ludger. 2003. "Labour Migration, Social Incorporation and Transmigration in the New and Old Europe: The Case of Germany in a Comparative Perspective." *Transfer: European Review of Labour and Research* 9 (3): 432–51.

Pun, Ngai, and Chris Smith. 2007. "Putting Transnational Labour Process in Its Place: The Dormitory Labour Regime in Post-Socialist China." *Work, Employment & Society* 21 (1): 27–45.

Radaelli, Claudio, and Romain Pasquier. 2006. "Conceptual Issues." In *Europeanization: New Research Agendas*, edited by P. Graziano and M. P. Vink, 35–45. Basingstoke, Hampshire: Palgrave Macmillan.

Raess, Damian, and Brian Burgoon. 2013. "Flexible Work and Immigration in Europe." *British Journal of Industrial Relations* 53 (1): 94–111.

Rainnie, Al, Susan McGrath-Champ, and Andrew Herod. 2010. "Making Space for Geography in Labour Process Theory." In *Working Life: Renewing Labour Process Analysis*, edited by Paul Thompson and Chris Smith, 297–316. Basingstoke, UK: Palgrave Macmillan.

Refslund, Bjarke. 2012. "Offshoring Danish Jobs to Germany—Regional Effects and Challenges to Workers' Organisation in the Slaughterhouse Industry." *Work Organisation, Labour & Globalisation* 6 (2): 113–29.

Refslund, Bjarke, and Ines Wagner. 2018. "Different Possibilities for Workers' Solidarity in the Danish-German Transnational Slaughterhouse Industry." In *Reconstructing Solidarity: Labour Unions, Precarious Work, and the Politics of Institutional Change in Europe*, edited by V. Doellgast, N. Lillie, and V. Pulignano, 67–83. Oxford: Oxford University Press.

Roberts, Bryan R., Reanne Frank, and Fernando Lozano-Ascencio. 1999. "Transnational Migrant Communities and Mexican Migration to the US." *Ethnic and Racial Studies* 22 (2): 238–66.

Rokkan, Stein. 1999. *State Formation, Nation-Building and Mass Politics in Europe: The Theory of Stein Rokkan.* Oxford: Oxford University Press.

Ruggie, John G. 1993. "Territoriality and Beyond: Problematizing Modernity in International Relations." *International Organization* 47 (1): 139–74.

Rumford, Chris. 2008. *Citizens and Borderwork in Contemporary Europe.* London: Routledge.

Rußig, Volker. 1996. "Bauwirtschaft in Deutschland: Beschleunigter Strukturwandel" [Construction industry in Germany: Accelerated structural change]. *Ifo Schnelldienst* 49 (11): 3–12.

Samers, Michael. 2003. "Invisible Capitalism: Political Economy and the Regulation of Undocumented Immigration in France." *Economy and Society* 32 (4): 555–83.

Sassen, Saskia. 2005. "When National Territory Is Home to the Global: Old Borders to Novel Borderings." *New Political Economy* 10 (4): 523–41.

Scharpf, Fritz W. 1999. *Governing in Europe: Effective and Democratic?* Oxford: Oxford University Press.

Scharpf, Fritz W. 2006. "The Joint-Decision Trap Revisited." *Journal of Common Market Studies* 44 (4): 845–64.

Scharpf, Fritz W. 2008. "Der einzige Weg ist, dem EuGH nicht zu folgen" [The only way is not to follow the ECJ]. *Mitbestimmung* 7 (8): 18–23.

Shire, Karen, Steffen Heinrich, Jun Imai, Hannelore Mottweiler, Markus Tünte, and Chih-Chieh Wang. Forthcoming. "Private Labour Market Intermediaries in Cross-Border Labour Markets in Europe and Asia: International Norms, Regional Actors, and Patterns of Cross-Border Labour Mobility."

Siebenhüter, Sabine. 2013. *Werkverträge in Bayern: Das neue Lohndumping-Instrument* [Subcontracts in Bavaria: The new wage dumping instrument]. Munich: Deutscher Gewerkschaftsbund.

Silver, Beverly J. 2003. *Forces of Labor: Workers' Movements and Globalization since 1870.* New York: Cambridge University Press.

Smith, Chris. 2003. "Living at Work: Management Control and the Chinese Dormitory Labor System." *Asia Pacific Journal of Management* 20 (3): 333–58.

Smyth, Russell, Xiaolei Qian, Ingrid Nielsen, and Ines Kaempfer. 2011. "Working Hours in Supply Chain Chinese and Thai Factories: Evidence from the Fair Labor Association's 'Soccer Project.'" *British Journal of Industrial Relations* 51 (2): 382–408.

Spencer, Sarah, Martin Ruhs, Bridget Anderson, and Ben Rogaly. 2007. *Migrants' Lives beyond the Workplace: The Experiences of Central and East European Migrants in the UK.* The Homestead: Report funded by the Joseph Rowntree Foundation.

Staggenborg, Suzanne. 1986. "Coalition Work in the Pro-Choice Movement: Organizational and Environmental Opportunities and Obstacles." *Social Problems* 33 (5): 374–90.

Stake, Robert E. 1995. *The Art of Case Study Research.* London: SAGE.

Steen Knudsen, Jette. 2005. "Is the Single European Market an Illusion? Obstacles to Reform of EU Takeover Regulation." *European Law Journal* 11 (4): 507–24.

Stobbe, Holk. 2002. *Undokumentierte Migration in Deutschland und den Vereinigten Staaten: Interne Migrationskontrollen und die Handlungsräume von Sans Papier* [Undocumented migration in Germany and the United States: Internal migration controls and the scope of action of Sans Papier]. Göttingen: Universitätsverlag Göttingen.

Streeck, Wolfgang. 1992. "National Diversity, Regime Competition and Institutional Deadlock: Problems in Forming a European Industrial Relations System." *Journal of Public Policy* 12 (4): 301–30.

Streeck, Wolfgang. 2003. "From State Weakness as Strength to State Weakness as Weakness: Welfare Corporatism and the Private Use of the Public Interest." MPIfG Working Paper 03/2. Max Planck Institute for the Study of Societies, Cologne, Germany.

Streeck, Wolfgang. 2009. *Re-forming Capitalism: Institutional Change in the German Political Economy.* Oxford: Oxford University Press.

Streeck, Wolfgang. 2011. "Taking Capitalism Seriously." *Socio-Economic Review* 9 (1): 137–67.

Streeck, Wolfgang, and Anke Hassel. 2003. "Trade Unions as Political Actors." In *International Handbook of Trade Unions,* edited by J. T. Addison and C. Schnabel, 335–65. Cheltenham: Edward Elgar.

Streeck, Wolfgang, and Kathleen Thelen. 2005. *Beyond Continuity: Institutional Change in Advanced Political Economies.* Oxford: Oxford University Press.

Studer, Brigitte. 2001. "Citizenship as Contingent National Belonging: Married Women and Foreigners in Twentieth-Century Switzerland." *Gender & History* 13 (3): 622–54. doi:10.1111/1468-0424.00246.

Supiot, Alain. 2009. "The Territorial Inscription of Laws." In *Soziologische Jurisprudenz, Festschrif für Gunther Teubner* [Sociological prudence, commemorative publication for Gunther Teubner], 375–93. Berlin: De Gruyter.

Tapia, Maite, and Lowell Turner. 2013. "Union Campaigns as Countermovements: Mobilizing Immigrant Workers in France and the United Kingdom." *British Journal of Industrial Relations* 51 (3): 601–22.

Taylor, Phil. 2010. "The Globalization of Service Work: Analysing the Transnational Call Centre Value Chain." In *Working Life: Renewing Labour Process Analysis*, edited by Paul Thompson and Chris Smith, 244–68. Basingstoke, Hampshire: Palgrave Macmillan.

Thelen, Kathleen. 2000. "Timing and Temporality in the Analysis of Institutional Evolution and Change." *Studies in American Political Development* 14 (1): 101–8.

Thelen, Kathleen. 2004. *How Institutions Evolve: The Political Economy of Skills in Germany, Britain, the United States and Japan*. New York: Cambridge University Press.

Thelen, Kathleen. 2009. "Institutional Change in Advanced Political Economies." *British Journal of Industrial Relations* 47 (3): 471–98.

Torpey, John. 1998. "Coming and Going: On the State Monopolization of the Legitimate 'Means of Movement.'" *Sociological Theory* 16 (3): 239–59.

Tsoukala, Anastassia. 2005. "Looking at Immigrants as Enemies." In *Controlling Frontiers: Free Movement into and within Europe*, edited by Didier Bigo and Elspeth Guild, 161–91. Aldershot, UK: Ashgate.

Turner, Lowell. 2009. "Institutions and Activism: Crisis and Opportunity for a German Labour Movement in Decline." *Industrial & Labour Relations Review* 62 (3): 294–312.

Unger, Brigitte, ed. 2015. *The German Model: Seen by Its Neighbours*. Brussels: Social Europ/SE Publishing.

Van Apeldoorn, Bastiaan. 2009. "The Contradictions of 'Embedded Neoliberalism' and Europe's Multi-level Legitimacy Crisis: The European Project and Its Limits." In *Contradictions and Limits of Neoliberal European Governance: From Lisbon to Lisbon*, edited by Bastiaan van Apeldoorn, Jan Drahokoupil, and Laura Horn, 21–43. Basingstoke, Hampshire: Palgrave Macmillan.

Vandaele, Kurt, and Janine Leschke. 2010. *Following the 'Organizing Model' of British Unions? Organizing Non-standard Workers in Germany and the Netherlands*. Brussels: ETUI Working Paper 2010.02.

Van Hoek, Aukje, and Mijke Houwerzijl. 2011. *Comparative Study on the Legal Aspects of the Posting of Workers in the Framework of the Provision of Services in the European Union*. Study to the European Commission Contract Number VT/2009/0541, 2011.

Van Maanen, John. 1988. *Tales of the Field: On Writing Ethnography*. Chicago: Chicago University Press.

Verstraete, Ginette. 2001. "Technological Frontiers and the Politics of Mobility in the European Union." *New Formations* 43: 26–43.

Visser, Jelle. 1996. "Internationalism in European Trade Unions: A Lost Perspective or a New Agenda?" In *The Lost Perspective? Trade Unions between Ideology and Social*

Action in the New Europe, vol. 2, edited by P. Pasture, J. Verberckmoes, and H. De-Witte, 176–79. Aldershot, UK: Ashgate.

Vogel, Berthold. 2004. *Leiharbeit. Neue sozialwissenschaftliche Befunde zu einer prekären Beschäftigungsform* [Temporary work: New social science findings on a precarious form of employment]. Hamburg: VSA-Verlag.

Voss-Dahm, Dorothea. 2008. "Low Paid but Committed to the Industry: Salespeople in the Retail Sector." In *Low Wage Work in Germany*, edited by G. Bosch and C. Weinkopf, 253–87. New York: Russell Sage Foundation.

Waddington, David. 1994. "Participant Observation." In *Qualitative Methods in Organizational Research*, edited by C. Cassell and G. Symon, 107–22. London: Sage.

Wagner, Bettina, and Anke Hassel. 2016. "Posting, Subcontracting and Low-Wage Employment in the German Meat Industry." *Transfer: European Review of Labour and Research* 22 (2): 163–78.

Wagner, Ines. 2015a. "The Political Economy of Borders in a 'Borderless' European Labour Market." *Journal of Common Market Studies* 53 (6): 1370–85.

Wagner, Ines. 2015b. "Rule Enactment in a Pan-European Labour Market: Transnational Posted Work in the German Construction Sector." *British Journal of Industrial Relations* 53 (4): 692–710.

Wagner, Ines. 2015c. "EU Posted Work and Transnational Action in the German Meat Industry." *Transfer: European Review of Labour and Research* 21 (2): 201–13.

Wagner, Ines. 2017. "Trade Unions and Migrant Workers in Germany: Unions between National and Transnational Labour Market Segmentation." In *Trade Unions, Immigration and Immigrants in Europe in the 21st Century: New Approaches under Changed Conditions*, edited by S. Marino, R. Penninx, and J. Roosblad, 158–78. Cheltenham, UK: Edward Elgar.

Wagner, Ines, and Lisa Berntsen. 2016. "Restricted Rights: Obstacles in Enforcing the Labour Rights of Mobile EU Workers in the German and Dutch Construction Sector." *Transfer: European Review of Labour and Research* 22 (2): 193–207.

Wagner, Ines, and Nathan Lillie. 2014. "European Integration and the Disembbeding of Labour Market Regulation: Transnational Labour Relations at the European Central Bank Construction Site." *Journal of Common Market Studies* 52 (2): 403–19.

Wagner, Ines, and Bjarke Refslund. 2016. "Understanding the Divergent Trajectories of Slaughterhouse Work in Germany and Denmark: A Power Resource Approach." *European Journal of Industrial Relations* 22 (4): 335–51.

Wagner, Ines, and Karen Shire. 2018. "Posted Work as a Migration Industry: The European Union and Asia compared." Conference paper prepared for the Council of European Studies Conference, 2018, Chicago.

Waldinger, Roger D., and Michael I. Lichter. 2003. *How the Other Half Works: Immigration and the Social Organization of Labor*. Berkeley: University of California Press.

Weber, Max. 1947. *The Theory of Social and Economic Organization*. Translated by T. Parsons and A. M. Henderson. Glencoe, IL: Free Press & Falcon's Wing.

Weber, Max. 1994. "The Nation State and Economic Policy." In *Political Writings*, 1–29. Cambridge: Cambridge University Press.

Wehler, Hans-Ulrich. 2008. *Deutsche Gesellschaftsgeschichte: 1949–1990* [A German social history: 1949–1990]. Munich: C. H. Beck.

Weinkopf, Claudia, Bettina Hieming, and Leila Mesaros. 2009. Prekäre Beschäftigung: Expertise für die SPD-Landtagsfraktion NRW [Precarious employment: Expertise for the SPD parliamentary group NRW (North Rhine Westphalia)]. Duisburg, Germany: Institut Arbeit und Qualifikation.

Wills, Jane. 2004. "Organising the Low Paid: East London's Living Wage Campaign as a Vehicle for Change." In *The Future of Worker Representation*, edited by G. Healy, E. Heery, P. Taylor, and W. Brown, 264–82. Basingstoke, Hampshire: Palgrave Macmillan.

Wilpert, Czarina. 1998. "Migration and Informal Work in the New Berlin: New Forms of Work or New Sources of Labour?" *Journal of Ethnic and Migration Studies* 24 (2): 269–94.

Woll, Cornelia, and Sophie Jacquot. 2010. "Using Europe: Strategic Action in Multi-level Politics." *Comparative European Politics* 8 (1): 110–26.

WZB Datenreport. 2011. *Ein Sozialbericht für die Bundesrepublik Deutschland* [A social report for the Federal Republic of Germany]. Bonn, Germany: Bundeszentrale für politische Bildung [Federal Agency for Political Education].

Yin, Robert K. 2006. *Case Study Research: Design and Methods*. 4th ed. Thousand Oaks, CA: SAGE.

Zentralverband deutsches Baugewerbe (ZDB). 2006. *Hintergrund zum Thema Schwarzarbeit und illegalBeschäftigung* [Background on illicit work and illegal employment]. Berlin: ZdB.

Zielonka, Jan. 2000. "How New Enlarged Borders Will Reshape the European Union." *Journal of Common Market Studies* 39 (3): 507–36.

Index

foreign worker schemes in, history of, 3, 4, 45–46; trade unions in, 18; unfair competitive practices of, complaints about, 51, 115; worker expectations vs. actual experience in, 1. *See also* construction industry; meat slaughtering industry; metal industry

Glick, William H., 24

Global Production Networks, 100

Global Value Chains, 100

Greer, Ian, 12, 122

group conversations, 24, 29

guest workers, in Germany, 45–46

Hacker, Jacob S., 33, 58, 70

Hartz reform package, 39

HDB (Hauptverband Deutsche Bauindustrie), 49–50

health and safety standards, undermining of, 63

Held, David, 17

Hirschman, Albert O., 39

holiday entitlements, withholding of, 61–62

host societies, posted workers' isolation from, 7–8, 10, 15, 78

housing sites, for posted workers: fire at, 120; management surveillance at, 83, 86, 90; participant observation at, 31; substandard conditions at, 83; visits to, 26–27

IG BAU (Industrie Gewerkschaft Bauen-Agrar-Umwelt), 49; initiatives to organize posted workers, 87–88; obstacles to interaction with posted workers, 67, 71–72

IG Metall (Industrie Gewerkschaft Metall): and collective agreements for posted workers, 80, 120; interviews with representatives of, 25

ILO. *See* International Labour Organization

immigration: and industrial relations institutions, 87; as labor-control issue, German law on, 102

industrial relations: comparative, 14–15; territorial principle and, 40–42. *See also* industrial relations institutions; national industrial relations systems

industrial relations institutions: immigration undermining, 87; posted workers excluded from, 35, 106, 108, 111; territorial

boundedness and efficient functioning of, 39, 76, 78, 108, 113. *See also* trade unions

industrial services, mobile labor in, 119

inequality, EU enlargement and new forms of, 63, 118; potential backlash against, 129

inspection. *See* labor inspection

institution(s): actors' relationship to, 16, 58; borders as, 20, 101; definition of, 69; strategic responses of organizations to, 71. *See also* industrial relations institutions; institutional change

institutional change: contribution to theory of, 15–16; different modes of, 70–72; foreign actors as missionaries of, 16; vs. functional change, 126; and loopholes exploited by management, 73; microlevel power dynamics and, 33, 57–59, 72, 116

International Labour Organization (ILO), Convention 94 of, 8

interviews, 3, 13, 24, 25; coding of, 32, 33, 34; interpreters used in, 29–30; location of, 29; of native workers, 30; overview of, 133–34; of posted workers, 27–30; questions used in, 27–28; validation of data from, participant observation and, 31

intracorporate transfer directive, 128

Jaehrling, Karen, 53, 54, 74

Japan, and temporary-staffing industry in East Asia, 129

joint liability, 46–47

Jørgensen, Knut, 111

Katz, Cindi, 93

Katzenstein, Peter J., 112

Krings, Torben, 47, 77, 79

labor inspection: barriers to, 102–5; in Germany, 59–60; inability to detect malpractices, 61, 68–69, 72; proposed European agency for, 127. *See also* FKS

labor market: EU, unidirectional membranes in, 111–12; international vs. transnational, 7. *See also* dualization, labor market; pan-European labor market

labor migrants (migrant workers): agency of, 92–93, 109; coalitions in relation to, 95; exploitation of, 115, 119–20; income levels of, 44; institutionalized separation of, 45;

labor migrants *(continued)*
  intra-EU, exclusion from social protections,
  128–29; labor market segmentation and, 40;
  overrepresentation in precarious forms of
  work, 44–45; posted workers distinguished
  from, 7–8, 10, 17, 41; tolerance toward
  substandard working conditions, 65; trade
  unions' ability to organize, 18, 87–89; and
  unemployment, blame for, 4, 129. *See also*
  posted workers; temporary migrant
  workers
labor rights. *See* enforcement of labor rights;
  rights
language barriers, migrant workers and, 8,
  67, 81, 90; trade union efforts to address,
  68
Lannes, Xavier, 10
Laval case, 10, 11
layering, institutional, 70
Lillie, Nathan, 12, 121, 122
Lipsky, Michael, 58
logistics, mobile labor in, 119
Lozano Riera, Mariona, 6, 17

main contracting firm: liability of, push for,
  125; shaming of, 86, 90; and subcontracting
  firms, borders between, 2, 55–56, 80, 97,
  101, 106–8; and works councils, 79
management: circumvention of rules by,
  59–64, 73; de-territorialization and exit
  options for, 12, 15, 38, 39, 78–79; unions'
  and labor inspectors' inability to counter,
  73–74
Martin, Antonio, 6, 17
MAXQDA software, 32
Meardi, Guglielmo, 6, 17
meat slaughtering industry, German, 51–54;
  boundaries between main contractor and
  subcontractors in, 55–56; employer
  associations in, 53; exploitative working
  conditions in, 51, 83, 115; gender distribution of workers in, 28; migrants overrepresented in, 44; minimum wage in, 53–54;
  positive changes in, 123–24; posted workers
  in, 51, 52; posted workers in, case study of,
  77–78, 82–87, 90–95; posting in, prevalence
  of, 3; Posting Law and, 46, 47, 54; selection
  for case studies, 24; structural changes in,
  51–52; subcontracting arrangements in,

36–37, 52–53, 54, 107; union in, 52, 53;
  wages of posted workers in, 66, 106
media: and agenda-building, 91; on substandard
  conditions for posted workers, 84, 85–86,
  90, 123
Méhaut, Patrick, 74
membranes, borders as, 111–12
Menz, Georg, 14
metal industry, German: collective agreements in, posted workers included in, 80,
  120; outsourcing in, trend toward, 120;
  works councils in, 80. *See also* IG Metall
Meyer Werft, 80, 120
migrant labor: attractiveness to transnational
  capital, 89; as hyper-flexible buffer, 6;
  impact on society at large, 129; union policy
  on, 113; Weber on, 4. *See also* labor
  migrants
Mills, Colleen, 66
minijobs, 39, 74
minimum wage: vs. collective agreement
  wages, 106; in German construction
  industry, 50; in German meat industry,
  53–54; German Posting Law on, 46;
  management strategies for circumventing,
  60–64, 69; PWD on, 4; statutory, in
  Germany, 46–47, 50
mobile labor. *See* migrant labor
mobilization, of contingent/posted workers:
  case study of, 90–93; similarities in
  different country contexts, 93–94

national industrial relations systems: ECJ
  decisions undermining, 11; firm borders
  separating workers from, 35; transnational
  workspaces and reduced power of, 15–17.
  See also trade unions; works councils
nation-state: borders and, 14; EU integration
  and, 20; posted workers' place within, 5;
  reshaping of, 97; and seasonal labor, Weber
  on, 4; territorial principle and, 40. *See also*
  state borders; territorial boundedness
native workers: employment conditions for,
  changing European labor market and,
  66–67; interviews of, 30; relationship with
  posted workers, 66, 109–10, 111
neomedieval model, of EU, 110
Netherlands: construction firms in, rule
  avoidance by, 122; as destination for posted